Good writers for young readers

Critical essays edited by

DENNIS BUTTS

for Tommy and Elinor

Hart–Davis Educational

Granada Publishing Limited
First published in Great Britain 1977 by
Hart-Davis Educational Limited
Frogmore, St Albans, Hertfordshire

ISBN 0 247 12798 1

Printed in Great Britain by The Campfield Press, St Albans

Contents

Introduction

As a form in its own right, children's literature may be said to have started in 1744 when John Newbery brought out *A Little Pretty Pocket-Book*, the first of some thirty titles that he published for the young. The first substantial studies of the form appeared in the latter part of the nineteenth century in such works as *What Books to Lend and What to Give* by Charlotte Younge and *Juvenile Literature As It Is* by Edward Salmon (though briefer kinds of commentary, by Sarah Trimmer and others, had appeared earlier).

In the twentieth century the range and importance of children's literature have increased by leaps and bounds, more spectacularly so in recent years. This 'explosion' produced a record number of new books for children in 1975, when 2,688 new titles were published. Meanwhile critical interest has spread widely. Literary studies, informed reviewing in periodicals, developments in the curricula of schools and colleges, and formal and informal meetings between parents, teachers, and writers have all contributed to the momentum.

The Newbery medal was founded in America in 1922 as an annual award for the most distinguished contribution to literature for children; and its counterpart in this country, the Carnegie medal, has existed since 1936. In America too the first periodical about children's books and reading, *The Horn Book Magazine*, began in 1924, to be followed on this side of the Atlantic by such magazines as *The Junior Bookshelf* (1936) and *The School Librarian* (1937). After the publication of F J Harvey Darton's broadly historical work *Children's Books in England* (1932), critical interest was sustained and extended by A J Jenkinson's survey of children's reading habits, *What Do Boys and Girls Read?* (1940), Geoffrey Trease's study *Tales Out of School* (1948), and Kathleen Lines' suggested library of books for children, *Four to Fourteen* (1950). But the most significant *single* development in children's book publishing during the last fifty years has almost certainly been the success of Puffins, the paperback series launched by Penguin Books in 1941. Edited at first by Eleanor Graham and then by Kaye Webb, Puffins first made good books widely available to children cheaply, attractively, and over a broad range of reading interests. More than nine million Puffins are now sold every year. Other popular paperback series have come to share the field, and some hardback publishers–such as Faber and Oxford–have begun to bring out their established books for children in paperback editions.

Since the last war good writers for young readers have appeared in non-stop profusion–Lucy Boston, Cynthia Harnett, C S Lewis, William Mayne, Mary Norton, Philippa Pearce, and Rosemary Sutcliff in the 1950s, Joan

4

Aiken, John Christopher, Leon Garfield, Alan Garner, Russell Hoban, and Kathleen Peyton in the 1960s, Richard Adams, Susan Cooper, Penelope Lively, Ursula LeGuin, and Ivan Southall in the 1970s, to name only the most prominent. At the same time government reports on education have repeatedly stressed the importance of literature in developing the sensibilities of children. As the Newsom Report on secondary education put it in 1963:

All pupils, including those of very limited attainments, need the civilising experience of contact with great literature. (Paragraph 473)

and the Plowden Report on primary education reaffirmed in 1967:

It is...through literature that children feel forward to the experiences, the hopes and fears that await them in adult life. (Paragraph 595)

The Bullock Report, *A Language for Life* (1975), devoted a whole chapter to the subject of literature's value in children's lives.

Magazines and periodicals devoted to the study of books for children have proliferated in the last fifteen years. *Growing Point* was started by Margery Fisher in 1962. It was soon joined by *Children's Book News*. In 1965 Anne Wood started *Books for Your Children* (and followed it up with the Federation of Children's Book Groups in 1968). In 1969 a national conference was held at St Luke's College, Exeter, on 'Recent Children's Fiction and its Role in Education'. This conference, attended by over 220 teachers, librarians, publishers, and writers, generated the magazine *Children's Literature in Education*, which originally appeared three times a year and is now published quarterly. Also in 1970 *Signal–Approaches to Children's Literature* was founded by Nancy Chambers, and was followed a year later by Valerie Alderson's *Children's Book Review*.

Particularly useful work that has appeared in book form since Frank Eyre's *20th Century Children's Books* (1952) includes the Bodley Head's series of monographs on individual writers, Margery Fisher's *Intent Upon Reading*, and John Rowe Townsend's *Written for Children* which appeared in 1965. In this book John Rowe Townsend eloquently voiced an enthusiasm and a sense of quality that growing numbers of adult readers of children's literature had been feeling. He wrote:

We always tend to think that there are not the great writers there used to be. Where, we ask, are the Stevensons and Nesbits and Grahames of today? The answer is that they are in our midst. I have no doubt that by the end of this century the great names of the 1950s and 1960s will stand out for all to see. There will be quite a number of them, and they will rank with the best of former times. The half century before 1914 was the first golden age of Children's Literature. The second golden age is now.

The reasons for this enthusiasm and these developments are, of course, complicated and in the last resort impossible to analyse. It is not too difficult, however, to relate some of them to the changes in British society over the last forty years. Higher standards of living for most people since 1945 have meant the purchase of more books, while new methods of publishing and distribution have made them more readily available than ever before. Radio, films, and television have helped to disseminate information about books and their authors. One thinks especially of recent visual interpretations of books like *The Railway Children*, *The Owl Service*, and the stories of Nina Bawden.

What is surprising, however, is not so much that the demand for children's books should have increased as a result of such varied socio-economic pressures, but that writers should have made such a whole-hearted response. It would be foolish to deny that some of them were influenced by the opportunity to win a lucrative audience, or that others turned to writing children's books when their ambitions as writers for adults were frustrated. But other reasons may also be found. Perhaps the pioneering influence of the 1930s and 1940s made the young readers of that time, who came to maturity themselves a generation later, aware of the possibilities inherent in good children's books. It may also be that in writing books for children some authors have found a form which enables them not only to re-experience the world of childhood but to awaken memories and state certainties which the adult has forgotten.

Despite the impressive nature of the achievements associated with children's literature since the 1950s, reservations do exist. In Eleanor von Schweinitz's challenging of 'The New Golden Age' in *Children's Book News* (May/June 1969), for example, she expresses concern about the quality of discussion surrounding children's literature. It is true that authors reviewing each other's books in the press may find it difficult to be severe with each other, especially if their own books may come up for review shortly! Nigel Hand states in his article on 'Criticism and the Children's Literature Industry' (*CLE*, vol 14) that the review columns of the 'quality' newspapers and weeklies are in the hands of 'an alliance composed of the critically incompetent and the authors themselves'. He may be overstating the case, but he is voicing a fairly widespread unease.

A second reservation about children's books in the last thirty years is concerned with the way in which certain kinds of authors and certain kinds of books, mainly historical novels and fantasies, have been almost predictably well received, as if they enshrined certain values and attitudes which of themselves automatically guaranteed their authors a place in the Pantheon of literary giants. The list of Carnegie prize-winners since the 1950s seems to provide many examples that would fit into this category, and may have had the result of perpetuating this kind of book.

Moreover, many people are beginning to feel that, although lavish praise has been heaped upon certain books by teachers and parents, the children for whom the books were written have been away reading something else. Even the ablest and most sophisticated children have, no doubt, always been able to read several different kinds of material, which operate at different levels and give different kinds of satisfaction, at the same time. The third-former who can enjoy reading Philip Larkin, *The Owl Service*, and the *Beano* on the same day is not unknown. But, as *Children's Reading Interests* (Evans/Methuen Educational, 1975) has shown, 29% of children at 14+ read comics only. This survey of the reading habits of 7800 children has thrown grave doubts on the popularity of many of the best authors, with this devastating paragraph:

Writers such as Joan Aiken, L M Boston, Meindert DeJong, Leon Garfield, Cynthia Harnett, William Mayne, Philippa Pearce, K M Peyton, Catherine Storr, Henry Treece, E B White and Laura Ingalls Wilder have been highly (and surely justly) praised by critics and children's librarians, and have even, in some cases given rise to the suggestion that the present day may come to be regarded as a 'Golden Age' of children's literature. Yet their books figured infrequently in the questionnaires, nor was there evidence of very wide reading even of the more firmly established children's writers such as Alan Garner, Rosemary Sutcliff or Arthur Ransome.

(Op cit, pp 32–3)

The most widely-read novel among children of 14+, in fact, sharing first place with *Little Women*, was Richard Allen's *Skinhead*. Here is a scene from the novel, in which the hero Joe Hawkings, who finishes up in prison for attacking a policeman, visits his girl-friend Sally:

'Marry me, Joe...'
He stiffened. 'You're crazy, Sally. We ain't old enough.'
'I'd run away with you, Joe...'
'Christ,' he exploded. 'You're fourteen, Sally!'
'And I take the Pill so you can...'
'Jeeze, I know that, doll.'
'Don't that mean somethin'?'
'Yeah, crawl over me. I'm getting the urge again...'
Her body flowed through his greedy hands, her thighs straddling him.
'Cor...' He kissed a breast, hands actively working between her thighs.
She bent over him, positioning herself...all fourteen years of experience doing what came naturally on their Tuesday.
'I'm ready,' Joe whispered.
She sank on to him, loving the feel of his penis buried in her body.
(Richard Allen, *Skinhead*, New English Library 1970)

The popularity of books like *Skinhead*, which sold over 200,000 copies in eighteen months, together with the arrival on the market of comics like *Warlord*, with its heavy concentration on violence, are seen by many people as reflecting some kind of failure by the authors of the Pantheon, who are felt to be too remote from the concerns and daily lives of many young potential readers. For some years, in fact, partly in order to help under-privileged children to learn to read more easily, books with industrial and urban rather than pastoral and middle-class settings have been published. Many attempts have been made to provide a literature which deals with some of the problems of adolescence, such as the tensions of parent-child relationships or the vicissitudes of early sexual encounters. And whether these books are written with conscious didactic aims or simply because they contain good stories, such work as Leila Berg's series of *Nippers*, Macmillan's *Topliners*, and some of the novels of Josephine Kamm (like *Young Mother*) do represent a modest kind of counter-culture within the tradition.

In 1975, moreover, the Children's Rights Workshop launched its own Other Award, presumably as an alternative children's book award to the Carnegie Prize. The Other Award is presented for the kind of book that, as well as having literary merit, deals with life as most of us know it, is free of the explicit or implicit values of competitive individualism, is historically accurate where appropriate, and shows a realistic and balanced depiction of sex roles. Bernard Ashley's *The Trouble with Donovan Croft*, commended for the Other Award in 1976, is the story of a working-class family who foster a West Indian boy, Donovan, because his mother has to go back to Jamaica. He and their son, Keith, go to junior school together, but the shock of being fostered out and apparently rejected by his parents causes Donovan to lose the power of speech. Accused of dumb insolence, he gets into many diffi-culties and tries to run away in his misery, before he recovers his voice when he sees his friend Keith in danger and needs to warn him.

The trouble with such books, for all their decent human values and their painstaking attempts at realism, is that they often seem to confuse good intentions with the successful execution of them in literary terms. This atti-tude often leads to what Elaine Moss has called 'bibliotherapy'–'You have a problem? I think this book should help you'–and this can often result in the relationship between literature and the reader being treated in a simplistic and reductive way. This kind of book also tends to identify 'life as most of us know it' with the descriptive reproduction of urban and industrial scenes. The danger of this is that, while realistic fiction may help us and posterity to understand the workings of late twentieth-century industrial situations, it may not be able to tell us what living then actually felt like or what individual writers of genius thought about it.

In his book *Ideology and the Imagination* (CUP, 1975), for example, Fred

Inglis has argued that many of the children's classics of the past–*The Wind in the Willows, Puck of Pook's Hill,* and *King Solomon's Mines* are three he specifies–asserted the superiority of various values: ideals of duty and loyalty to the state, the importance of individual choice, and certain ideas about the individual self. Modern reality, he then goes on to argue, has made it harder to maintain such values, and writers will have to search to find new forms of literature in order to express the newly-emerging values, including that of goodness itself.

For such developments it may be that the neo-realistic novel, even when written by teenagers themselves like *The Gates* by Leslie Mildner and Bill House, will not be enough. Ted Hughes' myth, *The Iron Man,* may be the best account of the anxieties and potentialities which our industrial society is capable of expressing at this time, and Russell Hoban's story of a talking clockwork toy, *The Mouse and His Child,* the best portrayal of man's search to realise his humanity in a society that seeks first to alienate him and then to destroy his identity and freedom.

What, therefore, emerges very clearly, as one begins to talk about the successes and failures of the second golden age of children's literature, is a good deal of uncertainty about the methodology and criteria for talking about children's books.

This is not surprising, and one should be neither disconcerted nor disheartened at this stage. The rise of children's literature is a fairly recent phenomenon and attempts at criticism even more recent. So many different kinds of books are published for different kinds of children, and then reviewed and debated by so many different readers, teachers, psychologists, parents, fellow authors, that it would be extraordinary if there were not a diversity of approaches in what is a very individual matter anyway. Even so, as more time and thought are devoted to discussing children's literature, two or three different approaches seem to dominate.

Since much children's literature takes the form of narrative fiction, it would seem that the most logical critical approach to it would be that already adopted towards adult novels. It is not too difficult, for example, to compare the work of K M Peyton with that of Charlotte Brontë. But this approach on its own is not entirely satisfactory because it ignores the many necessary differences of literary form between many children's books and those for adults, even when they seem similar, as with novels, and it also ignores the matter of readership. How far adults can deal with literature not written for them in the first place is a question that has bothered many readers.

Faced with these difficulties, therefore, another approach to the discussion of children's books is based upon the argument that the only critical criteria which have any value are those based upon the response of the children themselves. (Some newspapers seem to support this view by asking children to write book reviews for them at particular times of the year, like Christmas, when, they seem to imply, standards do not matter quite so much.) While this attitude has the merit of at least recognising the existence of readers, it can easily lead to the difficulties and inconsistencies pointed out in Bryan Alderson's fine, if provocatively-entitled, essay, 'The Irrelevance of Children to the Children's Book Reviewer' (*Children's Book News*, January/February 1969). He expresses the feeling, for example, that children often lack the power to articulate their responses to books clearly, and that, because of their inevitably limited literary experience, they may have difficulty in coping with new forms, unless skilfully led into them by adults.

Because of the limitations of these approaches towards the discussion of children's books, a third approach, although not yet clearly articulated, is gradually appearing, based upon the recognition of children's books as a literary *genre*. This approach regards children's books as a sub-division of literature proper, like, for example, the pastoral elegy, with its own conventions and characteristics, which are neither good nor bad in themselves, but exist only as the framework by which the author expresses his view of life. Value judgments derive, therefore, from trying to assess the writer's point of view and how successfully he used the conventions to express it, as with other forms of literature, and without criticising a work for following the conventions of its *genre*.

Among the characteristics of the *genre* of children's fiction, for example, are such obvious factors as the presence of child-protagonists, greater flexibility about the probability of narrative events, and recurring plot-elements such as the quest, the journey through time, falls and rises of fortune, and various kinds of initiation into adult life. Because of children's immaturity, some linguistic, emotional, and intellectual limitations are inherent in the *genre*, though this is by no means certain. Few people, for example, would once have expected sexual relationships to have been dealt with so sensitively in a children's book as they are in Paul Zindel's *I never Loved your Mind*. And indeed Myles McDowell has argued in a recent essay in *Children's Literature in Education* ('Fiction for children and adults', March 1973) that while an adult novelist might draw attention to the complexity of experience in a fairly raw way, and leave the reader to draw his own conclusions and comfort, a good children's writer will also make that complex experience available but perhaps in a slightly different, more guarded way. This is clearly an aspect of *genre*-theory which needs further clarification, but its defenders would argue that all *genres* have some limitations, such as the realistic novel's inability to deal with fantasy or farce's rejection of grief.

Such an approach, based on treating children's books as a *genre*, enormously influenced by its readers, but essentially a literary form in its own right, might help to explain the way in which some authors–Joan

Aiken, Nina Bawden, and Russell Hoban to name only three–seem able to turn easily from writing adult novels to writing children's books. It may also throw some light on the way some books, like *Watership Down*, for example, have fluctuated on publishers' lists between children's and adult fiction. These are clearly very adult writers using or preferring to work in the form of the children's book from time to time. As Graham Greene has used the form of the thriller or detective story to explore his tragic and religious view of life, it seems very likely that other writers have chosen to write and are writing children's stories now 'because', in the words of C S Lewis, 'a children's story is the best art form for something you have to say: just as a composer might write a Dead March not because there was a public funeral in view but because certain musical ideas that occurred to him best went into that form' (R L Green, *C S Lewis*, The Bodley Head, 1963).

There is clearly a need for much more discussion in this whole area of critical approaches, for there are many questions to be answered. How satisfactory is the *genre* theory? To what extent will this theory be able to deal with the new kinds of books Fred Inglis anticipates, which may break the conventions of children's fiction as violently as the music of Schoenberg and Stravinsky broke with what went before? What contribution to these discussions can be made by the criticism of Lukacs and Goldman, or the work by Malte Dahrendorf and Dieter Richter, for example, which is now coming out of Germany? To what extent, in fact, can children's literature be exposed to the whole apparatus of literary criticism?

From its earliest days *The Use of English* magazine has taken both children's literature and these kinds of questions very seriously. This magazine, primarily concerned with discussing the teaching of English in schools, contained an article in its very first number (in its revised form) by Boris Ford on 'The Reading Habit' (Autumn, 1949). Through reviews, articles, and exchanges like those on 'Secondary Modern Fiction' between E W Hildick and David Holbrook in the 1950s, it has kept its readers well-informed and alert to the problems and challenges of literature in general and new children's books in particular. By the 1960s the series on 'Writers for Children', from which most of the essays in this volume are chosen, had been launched. This kept its readers informed of new developments and reflected a whole range of critical responses.

Most of the essays printed here therefore reflect the range of criticism of children's literature published in *The Use of English* over the last decade. A few essays are printed here for the first time. Each of them contains a book list. Guides to further reading and some additional book lists of a more general kind are provided at the end.

DENNIS BUTTS

Joan Aiken's Historical Fantasies

by

LESLEY AERS

JOAN AIKEN's first three novels form a sequence, and as they also seem to me to develop interestingly in points of style and technique, it seems sensible to look at each one in turn, in the order in which they were written. In the first one, *The Wolves of Willoughby Chase*, various features of her method emerge in the early stages. There is the element of complete fantasy, but it is never quite separated from a knowable world: the wolves invade the railway station as well as Willoughby Chase; and Simon—who is from the first a changeling-figure—shows that he is not unconnected with the world when he sells his geese at the market, and so transforms them into hard cash. Similarly, Miss Slighcarp is a demonic character, but she never fails to be a definite physical presence. We are always aware of her height and boniness, and at the beginning we learn that she is bald beneath her grey wig—a physical detail that sets her down, unequivocally, as a villain. This is a style of characterisation that becomes familiar in the novels: certain traits of character and appearance are selected, and emphasised or exaggerated. This peopling the novels with types does not make them in any way flat or uninteresting, and it helps to maintain the clear outline of the plot. The plots are highly stylised, and events move into each other in the most direct and simple way; so that, although a number of things may be happening at once, there is never any effect of confusion or complexity. Thus it is a frequent device for the characters—usually the good ones—to overhear what the others are plotting (Bonnie and Sylvia in the secret tunnel hear what Miss Slighcarp and Mr Grimshaw are saying; or, in *Black Hearts in Battersea*, Sophie hears Buckle and Midwink talking). For, as it is necessary for the good characters to know what the bad ones are up to, it is refreshing to have them do so in the simplest way, and without any effort to cover it with trappings of 'realism': the children in the story do not wonder at their luck that they are overhearing a vital conversation—and so we, too, accept it as a device that is completely in place in the style of the book. We do not think of saying, 'Isn't it unlikely that the children would be there at that time—and that the villains would be talking so freely?' any more than we would think of saying, as we watched *Twelfth Night*, 'Isn't it unlikely that Malvolio should talk to himself like that–and that Sir Toby and the others should make remarks out loud, without being discovered?' It is a question of tone, and of the style of artifice that the writer establishes at the beginning. In Joan Aiken's novels we accept, and appreciate, many factors that we might reject elsewhere–secret tunnels, fortunate escapes, amazing coincidences, and chance meetings–for these are all used consciously, as devices, and there is no attempt to exclaim over them, or explain them away, or attach great significance to them. These kinds of happenings are part of the stylised pattern that is created in the novels.

This stylisation of plot and character informs the background of the stories also. In *The Wolves of Willoughby Chase* we have the great house, with its splendid park and rich furniture, and the toys that would be a child's paradise. Here is an idea of a breakfast-table in such a place:

Next morning the children had breakfast together in the nursery, which was gay with the sunshine that sparkled on crystal and silver and found golden lights in the honey and quince preserve.

Everything is simplified and exaggerated, but without ever making us feel that it is a different world that is being written about. Instead, it is a clarity, a transparency, that is conveyed. The same sort of perspective is aimed at in the account of Mrs Brisket's school: there is the same hint of cartoon-drawing, of defining the outlines, though maybe here we are closer to reality than the novel as a whole might lead younger readers to think. For the description of this school is not at all unlike Charlotte Brontë's impassioned account of Lowood in *Jane Eyre*, and some of Mrs Brisket's practices would have been all too familiar to those in charge of institutions and factories in the nineteenth century. The episode of the school is typical of the rest of the novel, however, in its characters–Mrs Brisket and her daughter Diana are perfect types of bullying and greed; and Bonnie's and Sylvia's eventual escape is carried out with the minimum of fuss. It is Simon who appears again to rescue them, as he did from the wolves on an earlier occasion. He leads them into an atmosphere of health; Sylvia recovers from the illness, which she developed at the school, as she travels bedded among Simon's geese, and when she stays in Mr Wilderness' lamb-filled barn. On their journey they see the world as natural, beautiful, awakening into spring; it is very different to Blastburn, where the school was, and 'where the huge slag-heaps stood outlined like black pyramids against a red sky'. This simple juxtaposition of beauty and degradation, of health and illness, offers ideas concisely–and realises them imaginatively–as a poem would do; and a child reading the novel would be aware of these processes at work.

Joan Aiken uses the wolves in her story to achieve a similarly simple, but poetic, effect. They establish right at the beginning a feeling of insecurity, which deepens into nightmare when the two girls are being chased by them –and it is Simon who provides the rescue. Against this background of danger, Miss Slighcarp and Mr Grimshaw come to Willoughby Chase. We are made to suspect Mr Grimshaw at the beginning, for he seems to have the look of a wolf:

'Excellent,' he remarked with a smile at Sylvia that bared every tooth in his head.

(One is reminded of this in *Night Birds on Nantucket*, when Dido Twite meets Miss Slighcarp and sees her as the wolf waiting for Little Red Riding Hood.) It is indeed a nightmare situation that then develops for Bonnie and Sylvia; especially for Bonnie, whose parents are exchanged for the wicked governess, who–worst of all–tries to assume the identity of Bonnie's mother, and wears her clothes. This transformation of the mother-figure would be more terrifying were it not for Bonnie's own resourcefulness; she is the first of Joan Aiken's competent–but also sensitive–heroines, who do not let themselves be oppressed by events. In the end, the nightmare lifts, and things are even better than they were at the beginning. Sylvia has grown too, in strength, and in the ability to cope, in the course of the book.

This idea of growth–of one character learning, and changing, in the process of the story, usually through the influence of another character–is shown clearly in the following novels as well. In *Black Hearts in Battersea* it is Dido Twite who changes, and again Simon is the influence of health. Dido at the beginning is a peevish, unattractive child, unloved by her family, and she is redeemed by Simon's sympathy and affection for her. All her good qualities are brought out as she comes to love him, and in the end she goes after him to rescue him from his captivity on the *Dark Dew*, and cares passionately for him when he is fevered, after the shipwreck. It is simple enough, the change that is wrought in Dido, but we are made to see, clearly, that all she ever needed was affection; her conversation here with Simon is, again, simple but moving:

Dido stirred and suddenly opened her eyes.
'Where's your kitty?' she muttered.
'I've lent it to a lady called Mrs Cobb.'
'Why?'
'To catch mice for her.'
Dido lay silent. Presently a large tear rolled out from under her closed eyelid.
'What's the matter?'
'First the donkey went–then the kitty went– next *you'll* go. I don't have anyone nice to play with–they allus leaves.'
'I shan't leave,' Simon soothed her. 'You go back to sleep.'

For the most part, however, Joan Aiken in this novel sacrifices the clear juxtapositions that she made in *The Wolves of Willoughby Chase*, in favour of a yet more outrageous plot, which she carries through with a Fielding-like gusto and delight in coincidences and reverses of fortune. Or perhaps it is more like Gilbert and Sullivan; every possible aspect of the situation is exploited–Simon, the unknown orphan, is the Duke's nephew; Sophie, his childhood friend (first brought up by an otter), turns out to be his sister; they both have the Battersea Tuft, and Sophie finds the bracelet that her mother gave her, which shows who she is; the villain had done some baby-swapping, and substituted his own son for the Duke's heir. There is no attempt–why should there be?–to make such events credible. Instead there is Joan Aiken's care to link all the details, and keep the pattern firm–thus it is always the Duchess's tapestry that saves her and the Duke's lives; it is only right that Simon should be shipwrecked on to Mrs Buckle's island, for she recognises him as the Duke's nephew, and Justin (the supposed heir) as her own son; the reason for Simon's artistic ability (and Justin's incompetence) becomes clear when Simon turns out to be the grandson of a great artist; the reason for the Duke's interest in balloons is clear when the balloon is needed in the end to rescue the characters from Battersea Castle. This close texture of the novel, which (as I have said before) does not become confusion, gives pleasure and satisfaction; a child would be aware of that. It is some of the unexpected elements within this pattern that give pleasure also; for instance, when Mrs Buckle treats her reunion with her son in a most practical fashion–and Justin is more upset to find that he is Mr Buckle's son than to find that he is *not* the Duke's heir. There is a robust humour at work here. We feel it also when Simon meets the disguised Mr Twite outside the castle. Mr Twite does not ignore Simon–as might be expected–but chats to him in a most friendly fashion; and we feel that it is right that Mr Twite escapes the explosion that engulfs the other villains, for at least he played the 'hoboy', if not very well. As in *The Wolves of Willoughby Chase*, characters are marked out by their idiosyncrasies; Mr Twite has his hoboy, the Duke his passion for mould, Dr Furneaux is the hot-tempered parody Frenchman, and the Duchess is always conscious of what is expected of a Duchess, whatever the situation.

Although the narrative itself shows clearness and restraint–note, for instance, the description of the explosion–it is in this novel that we first become particularly aware of Joan Aiken's playing with accents and language. This is not easy to do successfully; it could become repetitive and boring; but, as with the other features of the story, she carries it off with wit, changing and replacing familiar phrases engagingly. Here is Dr Furneaux at his best:

'Ah my poor sir, my dear friend!' he exclaimed, giving the Duke a bristly hug.

'How I commiserate wiss you. Your home lost–destructuated by zese brigands! Not zat I admired it–indeed, a most hideous building. But still, ze saying goes, does it not, ze Englishman's castle is his home?...'

There is also Dido's Cockney, which helps to dramatise her own particular resilience. In *Night Birds on Nantucket* we have Professor Breadno's splendid 'Wunderboots!' 'Köningsbang!' Such games with language are amusing in themselves, and, in a simple way, heighten our awareness of words.

After such extravagance in *Black Hearts in Battersea* (although the game–and in many ways it is a game–is always controlled), one wonders what will come next. In *Night Birds on Nantucket* the background is shifted, and yet more fantastical notions are combined in this story–far outstripping the use of the conventional fairy-tale idea behind Simon's history, the orphan who is the Duke's heir. In this third novel, we have Dido's ten-month sleep on the whaler, a gun that will shoot across the Atlantic, and a pink whale that loves the captain of the whaler; and all these are bound into one story with the closeness that is characteristic of all the novels. Other elements are characteristic too. There are the simplified identifiable personalities: we take Mr Slighcarp to be evil from his first appearance, when he says that the sleeping Dido should have been dropped overboard; on the other hand, we are never made to feel that Professor Breadno is wicked–Dido's sympathy for him, and his own child-like request for cake, forbid that. The judgment on him in the end is that his part in the plot has no malice in it–he only invented his huge gun out of a scientific curiosity; but the gun is just as dangerous, nevertheless. Miss Slighcarp herself, making her second appearance in Joan Aiken's sequence, is as cruel as before–her presence makes the whole atmosphere at the farm icy and unwelcoming–but she is different now in her fanaticism. Her death at the end, when she plummets over the cliff on the gun, is splendidly dramatic and unequivocal, and is only to be surpassed by Lord Malyn's appropriately Don Giovanni-like end in *The Whispering Mountain*. Evil tends to come to such final destruction in Joan Aiken's novels.

One almost has the sense, in *Night Birds on Nantucket*, that the author's imagination has finally run amok (why must the whale be *pink*?); but it is still held in place by the careful use, and linking, of details, and by the factors that are so completely recognisable, such as Dido's homesickness (although she knows that she won't be missed much at home), or the fact that Penitence, when she has shut herself up in the cupboard, can't resist the bowl of plum duff. Certainly I find this the most absorbing part of the novel, when Dido lures Penitence out of her hiding-place by her own natural vitality. For now it is Dido's turn to restore someone's character, and her own resourcefulness and robustness, which is so like that of Bonnie, Sophie, and Arabis, is set against Penitence's intense moping for her mother's death:

(Dido's) first attempt had met with no response; next time the only reaction had been a fierce, miserable whisper from behind the panel:

'Go away. Go *away*! Whoever you are I shan't come out. I know you're only trying to trick me to go up on deck and be drowned!'

Dido saw that she would have to be clever.

'What do you do all day long in there?' she asked, the beginnings of a plan sprouting in her mind. There was no answer. She had not really expected one. She went on, half to herself: 'Well, I don't wonder you gets blue-devilled if you does nothing but sit and think o' drowning all the time. Cheesy, *I* calls it!'

The theme of growth is carried on through the rest of the story, until at the end Penitence is a healthy child, freed of all the traumas and inhibitions that Dido had no patience with.

Although I feel that *Night Birds on Nantucket* is a success, I think it was a good thing that Joan Aiken abandoned the idea of a link with it when she embarked on her fourth novel (the first three novels are linked through character). This fourth novel, *The Whispering Mountain*, is striking in its freshness. It also seems as if Joan Aiken now has a complete, unforced assurance in her methods, for here we have the widest diversity of elements yet; but the hold on them does not falter, and they are kept in a clear relationship to each other. A whole variety of characters exist together, among them a lost Turkish tribe, a group of truculent Welsh boys, the King of England's son, and two Cockney thieves. We follow them in their movements between Pennygaff (for now we are in Wales), Nant Agerddau, Malyn Castle, or into the Whispering Mountain itself. People are brought together in different places and at different times, and move apart again, until finally, opera-like, everyone moves into one place and all the factors must sort themselves out at once.

There is in this novel, as in the others, the use of amazing chance happenings, and good fortune. After all, how could such disparate characters be held together in interrelationships, except by coincidences? It is, indeed, not a large number of people who play their parts in this novel, and the fact that they are all connected with each other, and continually meet each other, is the pattern of the story. The focus of their interest, the object that gives the final unity, is the lost harp.

In the first instance, Owen, who is being victimised by his school-fellows (it is an entirely recognisable situation–they are waiting to 'get him' after school), is fortunate to meet Mr Dando and his daughter Arabis. We learn that Owen has been with them before, when he was travelling to find his grandfather in Wales–here we see Joan Aiken applying her 'theory that it enriches a book to have had a lot of relevant action take place before the story opens'.* Later, we learn that the woman whom Lord Malyn once

* Joan Aiken 'A Thread of Mystery' *Children's Literature in Education*, 2 July 1970.

turned out into the snow to die was Arabis' mother, and this fact is the source of much unresolved tension. Arabis' mother was also a native of the island that the lost tribe came from. The links that Joan Aiken makes in *The Whispering Mountain* are of this kind, with a reference between times and places.

The kind of luck that Owen has in meeting Mr Dando's wagon, just when he needs help, follows him throughout, in spite of all the problems that befall him. Thus we never really doubt that he will escape from the ruined cottages–terrifying though his position is when he is held captive there; just as we never believe that the river will wash the boys away, when the waters rise; and Owen is fortunate to have his spectacles mended by Brother Ianto–and to discover in himself an unfailing skill with the crossbow. Not that his escapes happen in a predictable way, and it is here that much of the charm of the story resides. It is his Book of Knowledge that provides him with the answers–but it is his luck that leads him to find the creepers that are strong enough to bear the boys' weight across the gorge, or to hit the boar fair and square in the mouth, which his Book of Knowledge told him was his only hope. The Book of Knowledge (it is like the Duchess's tapestry in *Black Hearts in Battersea* in this way) helps Owen out of most of his tight corners: it provides vital and unexpected information; it provides the clue which leads Arabis to rescue Owen from the cottages; and it plays its final part when Owen drops it on the head of Lord Malyn's secretary, who falls off the rock into the Devil's Leap. This is all typical of Joan Aiken's stylisation of plot. We feel it is *right*–having become accustomed to her way of constructing a story, in which all features must interlock–when it turns out that Brother Ianto was at school with Owen's grandfather Mr Hughes, and that Miss Tegwyn Jones, who was, it seems, the last rightful owner of the harp, should have been Mr Dando's grandmother. One of the most humorous lucky escapes–this time Arabis'–which is not without its symbolic function, is when the wintergreen, that she had used to help the sick Children of the Pit, dopes the snakes that have been released into her dungeon.

Once more the characters are clearly marked out by certain traits, physical or otherwise. Arabis is certainly a girl of action; none of the children in Joan Aiken's novels are colourless cardboard figures who merely let strange things happen to them. They are always full of resistance and ingenuity. Arabis' action here, with its appropriate geographical detail, is typical of her briskness:

She kicked a loose rock under the rear wheel of the wagon so that it should not run away backwards downhill into the River Gaff.

Owen is characterised by his efficiency and knowledgeability–we can understand the dislike that he suffers from the other boys at the beginning! His talking is liberally supplemented by extracts from his Book:

'*Clematis vitalba*, or *virginiana*,' he explained. '"This beautiful plant, covered with white bloffoms, or furry fruit clufters, makes indeed a fitting bower for any maid or traveller who may chance to seek shelter. Leaflets are three-nerved from the bafe, entire or with a few coarfe teeth, hairy on the nerves—"'.

But Owen is far from being a buffoon; his feelings for his father are deep; he is loyal to his grandfather for as long as possible; and he bears the boys no grudge for their unkindness. It is a serious note when he chastises himself for having written the letters–though who would not, at knife-point? Yet he feels that Arabis would not.

Owen's grandfather is defined by his pig-headedness, but we are shown clearly, also, his moral courage. Tom Dando is the poet, preoccupied only with his poem. Abipaal is strange, surly, but marked by his intense fondness for music, and his fierce attachment to those who can make beautiful music– that is, here, Tom Dando and Arabis. Lord Malyn is a triumph of evil, yellow-eyed, dressed in black and gold like a wasp, his movements like an adder. Like Miss Slighcarp, he is thin, pale, a dominating presence. It seems appropriate at this point to put in a comment about Joan Aiken's names; from Lord Malyn to Captain Casket, they seem to be, almost all, unerringly chosen.

The Whispering Mountain certainly provided Joan Aiken with ample opportunity to play with language, and to use the different dialects which she obviously relishes. I do not think that this is a fault, for it is never boring, for there is life and not the forced artificiality that could have resulted, from this tactic. Briefly, here is an authentic Welsh tone–at least, it reminds me of *Under Milk Wood*, which is my, and most people's, only idea of Welsh voices:

'Mr Owen Hughes the museum, isn't it? Honoured we are, indeed. And what can I do for you, Mr Hughes? A drop of mead, will it be, to keep out the chill?'

The Seljuk's way of talking is amusing, and certainly 'readily recognisable', as Joan Aiken says. Similarly, the two thieves are obviously recognisable–so much so that we experience something of a shock when we hear their voices again, after believing them to be dead.

They are all killed at the ending, when the climax comes and the pattern is resolving itself into a triumph of good over evil. Their deaths are as dramatic and as total as Miss Slighcarp's in *Night Birds on Nantucket*. But the pattern is shaken; for the good fortune of the good characters, which, nevertheless, has never led us to exclude the unexpected, does not hold firm, and Tom Dando is killed in the struggle. He has at least completed his poem. His death is described characteristically, without fuss. The pattern re-forms to admit this harsher note, and in the final resolution Arabis, with Abipaal, and the harp, goes to live with Owen and Mr Hughes. We feel that Mr Hughes does deserve his part in the harmony; his good qualities were great, and he has come to a wiser understanding by the end of the book. Perhaps it is he, in this novel, who grows through his experiences; and so does Hwfa, who at the end is far from being the bully he was at the beginning.

As I have been trying to say, I believe it is a sense of shape that we are left with after reading the novel; such a sense as is a pleasure in its own right, and which has been created by the holding together of so many elements in a sustained and coherent pattern. All four novels are memorable for this shape, but *The Whispering Mountain* seems to contain more serious notes firmly within its compass.

(1971)

Postscript

Since this article was first printed, Joan Aiken has published two more novels, apart from a wealth of short stories. The first of the novels, *The Cuckoo Tree*, returns to the story of Hanoverian plots and the character of Dido Twite, who is again involved in incredible adventures, which she always manages to meet with a straight face. Indeed, it is this quality in the characters to be completely unperturbed by all the extraordinary events that befall them that is one of the novel's most endearing features. For instance, when Dido asks where Lord Forecastle lives:

'House in the Strand. How'll you get there?'
'Lord Sope lent me his elephant.'
'I was wondering where that came from,' Tethera said.

The elephant, who has learned to stop at the pubs on the road, excites little surprise from anyone; but of course this is the world of the earlier novels, with their wolves and whales, and anything can happen. In *The Cuckoo Tree* we not only have Lord Sope's elephant, but also the witch's rat who finds the vital document and chews it up, and a plot to make St Paul's Cathedral slide down the hill on giant rollers. The number of relatively normal characters seems to have shrunk even from the other books. Here we have witches, twins with amazing powers of communicating with each other, a sea captain in a coma, and Lady Tegleaze who is addicted to betting; but this mad world becomes recognisable when we meet the Home Secretary, who insists that it is impossible for Dido and her companions to get into the cathedral and warn the people of the danger, because they cannot get the necessary passes. Bureaucracy run mad *is* something we are used to.

The Cuckoo Tree is skilfully written and worked out, like the earlier novels, but there is perhaps too great a sense of *déjà vu* about it. Turning to *Midnight is a Place*, however, we are immediately aware of something very different, and more considerable. There is only the faintest of links with the other novels (*The Cuckoo Tree* even brings in, briefly, Owen Hughes from *The Whispering Mountain*): the town of Blastburn, in *Midnight is a Place*, is where Mrs Brisket's dismal school was in *The Wolves of Willoughby Chase*. But Blastburn is no longer just a brief episode. Joan Aiken explores the nature of the town and its work, and the effect this has on the people who live there. There is nothing gratuitously far-fetched about this novel; Joan Aiken has even given up her usual wealth of funny voices. Instead we are shown the different kinds of corruption that the town, and the carpet factory which dominates the town, produce. The carpet factory is brutal and dehumanised, and the machine is far more important than the individual: it produces brutal and dehumanised people, such as Bob Bludward, who exacts terrible penalties if people will not pay their dues to his 'Friendly Society'. Bob Bludward is half a machine himself; he rides round the factory in a mechanised wheelchair, and he shoots bolts with a deadly accuracy. We are not to be sorry for him. His physical injuries were inflicted by the machinery, but the psychological effect that the factory has had on him is much worse.

The struggle to survive in Blastburn produces other warped characters, such as the boy who extorts protection money from the relatives of hospital patients ('Last week they pull a poor old man out of his bed and leave him in the yard in the rain because his sons will not pay') and Mr Hobday, who employs a psychopath to collect any objects of value from the sewers for his market stall. Even characters who appear to be good, such as old Mr Scatcherd, have their taint: in the past, he received money for helping to deceive Sir Denzil and defraud him of his inheritance. Yet this allows Sir Denzil to escape the tentacles of Blastburn, even though he dies in poverty elsewhere, and Sir Randolph, who has tricked his way into the property, derives no pleasure from it and is finally driven mad, dying in the flames of his home which he has set alight. The trick he perpetrated on Sir Denzil was carried out by means of a bogus slice of Clutterby Pie. This may sound like the more typical Joan Aiken fantasia (wolves, whales, and elephants), but in *Midnight is a Place* the purpose is altogether more sombre.

Lucas, who had been assumed to be Sir Randolph's heir, is unhappy and withdrawn when the novel begins, unable to communicate his feelings except in letters to an imaginary friend. When he is left homeless and penniless after the fire, with Anna-Marie, the little half-French girl, he finds out what the town is really like, and what he is like too. In trying to make a living for himself, he even has to descend to the sewers to find goods for Mr Hobday, and is nearly killed there by Mr Hobday's murderous assistant. He is driven to the limits of his endurance, but he finds in himself–prompted by Anna-Marie–the capacity to care for other people.

Anna-Marie, like other girls in Joan Aiken's novels, is immensely energetic and resourceful. She refuses to be defeated by circumstances. She even takes work in the Mill to help earn some money. There she falls foul of Bob Bludward by insisting that people are more important than machines. He tries to murder her with the carpet-presser, and this is only too believable a death, as the novel begins with a girl being killed in the factory in this way.

But it is the people who stand up to events and learn to cope whom the novel celebrates. Lucas and Anna-Marie, keeping themselves and the injured Mr Oakapple alive; old Lady Murgatroyd, making a comfortable home in the old ice-house; Davey Scatcherd, doing what he can to improve conditions at the Mill, and dying for it in the end. And we are shown loyalty: the loyalty of Julian Oakapple to Sir Denzil and his family, and the loyalty of the children to Julian. When the evil faction from the Mill tries to flood the whole town, Lucas even runs to warn the mad Gudgeon, who had tried to murder him in the sewers, and Gudgeon replies with one of his texts: 'The end thereof shall come in a flood, but neither can the floods drown love.'

So it is strength and love that win, although the losses are real, such as the death of Davey Scatcherd. As Anna-Marie says: 'Well–he is dead–like Papa and Sidi. So that is that. But it is such a waste! He was so nice. And he p-played for the Blastburn Wanderers–'

The sense of loss amidst what has been won recalls *The Whispering Mountain* more than Joan Aiken's other novels. But *Midnight is a Place* goes beyond *The Whispering Mountain* in the kind of questions it explores. Like Owen Hughes, Lucas has a lot to learn, about himself and other people. He also has to learn about the nature of responsibility. Sir Denzil got away from Blastburn, but the Mill might have been a better place if he had tried to look after it. People need to work to live; the best thing is to make the conditions of work as pleasant as possible. Lucas will stay and do what he can in the Mill.

This is not a simple novel, and the reactions of the characters are not simple either. The Mill is evoked in details that are very realistic–and true to the working conditions in the early nineteenth century, especially for children–and yet Davey can say about Blastburn: 'Aye, it's a moocky old hole...There's a lot wrong, but still, it's lively! It gets a howd on ye, if ye live there.' As in the other novels, there is a multiplicity and rapidity of events and, again, coincidences, but Joan Aiken does not lose her hold on them. She has written a good story, and has created a satisfying pattern which still takes account of the complexity of life and our response to it. This is certainly her most impressive book for children so far.

LESLEY AERS

•

Books by Joan Aiken

Books for Children

Historical Fantasies

The Wolves of Willoughby Chase Cape, 1962
Black Hearts in Battersea Cape, 1966
Nightbirds in Nantucket Cape, 1966
The Cuckoo Tree Cape, 1971
Midnight is a Place Cape, 1974

Other Books

The Kingdom and the Cave Abelard-Schumann, 1957
Nightfall ('Topliners') Macmillan, 1969
The Bread Bin BBC Publications, 1974

Play

Winterthing and the Mooncusser's Daughter Cape, 1973

Collections

All You've Ever Wanted Cape, 1953
More Than You Bargained For Cape, 1955
A Necklace of Raindrops Cape, 1968
A Small Pinch of Weather Cape, 1969
All and More (a reprinting of All You've Ever Wanted and More Than You Bargained For)
    Cape, 1971
The Kingdom Under the Sea Cape, 1971
A Harp of Fishbones Cape, 1972
All But a Few Puffin Books, 1974
Tales of Arabel's Raven Cape and BBC Publications, 1974
A Bundle of Nerves Gollancz, 1976

Non-Fiction

Girls' Choice Hamlyn, 1969

The Novels of
L M Boston

by

PETER HOLLINDALE

MOST PEOPLE'S autobiographies are copious affairs. They set out to be complete statements of a lifetime, finding room and significance for every event and action: they tend to be both unselective in detail and shapely in outline, searching for patterns that crowding experience has obscured. An artist's autobiography often seems by comparison a limited work, high-lighting seemingly trivial details and leaving supposedly momentous events almost untouched. The motive of the book seems intrinsically different from that of, say, a politician, or soldier, or explorer: its business is not to discover patterns, because they already exist in accomplished work, but to declare the crucial obsessions that make the work such as it is and no other. The artist homes in on those parts of his life that in this way matter most, and shows up for inspection the living rock from which his work was hewn.

Lucy Boston's *Memory in a House*, by this criterion, is very much an artist's autobiography. In many ways it seems an inconsequential, shapeless, irritating book. Mrs Boston spends much time recounting her running battles with planning authorities, suspicious villagers, vandals, footballers, and tourists, and more in introducing us in intimate physical detail to her friends. Much space is given to the architectural restoration of her house and much to the garden–especially the roses. We are told about parties, and music, and boating or swimming in the nearby river, and grow warmly fond of Broomie the gardener. To anyone unfamiliar with Mrs Boston's other work, it will seem, perhaps, unusually interesting as a private domestic record, all the more so because of its author's wicked humour, alert observation, and uncompromising judgments, but distinctly odd in its priorities. It seems all the odder when we realise that Chapter I begins when the author is nearly fifty: the rest of life, including such supposedly interesting matters as her childhood in late-Victorian England, her work as a nurse in the First World War, her marriage and its break-up, and her life as a painter in Italy, Austria and Cambridge, is capriciously dismissed in a four-page prologue.

Mrs Boston is not, however, a domestic raconteur. As a person she distinguishes sharply between what is private and what is public; and privacy is something she cherishes. As an artist she knows what is germane to the understanding of her work and what is not. *Memory in a House* is a testament that life, *real* life, can begin anew and unexpectedly at any age: it is not so much the history of a life as the story of an obsession and the release of artistic imagination through love. Whether it seems trivial or serious, it contains almost nothing which is irrelevant to the genesis of Mrs Boston's novels, and contains important clues to the origins of many of them. The novels themselves form one of the most subtle, original and moving works of children's fiction in our times.

The house of the book's title is the Norman Manor of Hemingford Grey, near Cambridge, which Mrs Boston bought shortly before the Second World War and subsequently restored. It appears in one guise or another in nearly all her books, most notably as Green Knowe, in the six novels of a masterly sequence which is the centrepiece of Lucy Boston's work, and as Yew Hall in the novel of that title which appeared (when she was over sixty) as her first published book. It also appears in her story for younger children, *The Castle of Yew*, and in two of her shorter works, *The Guardians of the House* and *Nothing Said*. Only in two other shorter works, *The Sea Egg* and *The Fossil Snake*, is the setting elsewhere. (Incidentally, these last four titles should not be supposed because of their brevity to be designed for a different age-group from the *Green Knowe* series: *The Guardians of the House* is a kind of coda to the sequence, and *The Fossil Snake* repeats its preoccupation with the living continuity of past and present, while *The Sea Egg* and *Nothing Said* are partly lyric celebrations of sea and river, poetic, delicate and subtle.)

The insistence on a single setting may suggest a set of books which is claustrophobic and repetitious. In fact nothing could be less true–so little true, in fact, that each of the *Green Knowe* novels needs to be considered separately. The books are a sequence, but there are no 'sequels' except in the limited sense that the house and certain characters reappear. Mrs Boston has herself expressed the attitude of mind which permits such variety in unity. In *The Sea Egg*, where for once the setting *is* different, two small boys are removed for the day by well-meaning parents from the Cornish cove in which a newly magical world has opened up for them. The author comments: 'Their parents wanted for themselves the interest of a different seascape to look at. Also they mistakenly thought the boys would learn more by seeing more places.' (*The Sea Egg*, p 66.) This is not a mistake that the author herself has made. In a note she appended to the chapter about her in John Rowe Townsend's *A Sense of Story* she wrote: 'I am not a traveller, but have wandered in France, Italy, Austria and Hungary, and studied painting in Vienna. I believe that one place closely explored will yield more than continents passed through. Now I have found the place I need, and though postcards from abroad excite me to fever point, this is where I stay, getting deeper in it every moment and always surprised.' (*A Sense of Story*, p 36.)

A vital element in the success of the *Green Knowe* stories (and of Lucy Boston's other books) is their profound alertness to the spirit of place, their intimate astonished pleasure in its endless possibilities, their suggestion of amplitude and airy spaciousness in a seemingly confined locale, above all their sense of inheritance and continuity.

These qualities are true of all the *Green Knowe* stories, however great their individual differences, and the effect is important. The sense of variety and spaciousness comes in part from the nature of the house and its surroundings. At its heart is the Music Room or 'Knights' Hall', high and airy and shaped by time-absorbing stone, a coolly echoing hollowness of civilised interior space. The living room opens directly into the garden: not only do children move freely out but birds move freely in. House and garden support and continue each other. The garden itself has seemingly endless variety, creating its own harmony out of seclusion and diversity: there is a vegetable garden, there are roses, there are trees to climb, and there is a wood which is left untouched, as a sanctuary for wild things. It is a moated garden, and therefore inwardly protected, but part of it lies beyond the moat: its serenity is an enclave but not a fortress. Moat and garden in turn give way to river and fields; from these may come intruders, but they also offer a larger freedom to exploring children. Beyond, again, are the flat and watery fenland distances. The effect is of continuum, of a place that flows like water from its centre to horizons. Not for nothing is the house so often called the 'Ark': its natural element is as much water as land, and it offers both shelter and liberty to wild creatures and to children.

Green Knowe has other kinds of space to offer too. People as well as landscape link it with the outer world. Its owners, the Oldknow family, are not stay-at-homes. Of the four generations of Oldknow children who appear at times in the stories, only the twelfth-century Roger has a father regularly at home, and he is the original builder. Captain Oldknow, father of the seventeenth-century children, Toby, Alexander, and Linnet, is a sailor, and so is another Captain Oldknow, father of blind Susan at the end of the eighteenth century. The contemporary Oldknow child, Tolly, whose Christmas holiday with his great-grandmother in *The Children of Green Knowe* begins the series, has a father and stepmother in Burma. Even Roger d'Aulneaux, who has both his parents present, is isolated by his mother's indifference. So the pattern across the centuries is for the Oldknow children to be in some sense parentally neglected, even if the neglect is inadvertent or inescapable. They turn, as a rule, for consolation to a sympathetic grandmother, and to the house itself, which offers in its security and its challenges something of a parent's role. It is a very protective, hospitable dwelling to those who wish it well.

The freedom of Green Knowe is not confined to those who have dynastic rights as Oldknow children. It is a haven for the orphaned and 'displaced'. The black West Indian boy, Jacob, who is brought to Green Knowe by the eighteenth-century Captain Oldknow as a servant-companion for blind Susan, wins his way to a permanent home at the Manor; as a fugitive slave-child he is one of the 'displaced'. In the twentieth century, others follow. In that rather odd novel, *The River at Green Knowe*, the house is let for the summer, and its crackpot female tenants are inspired to offer a holiday welcome to two 'displaced' children, Oskar from Poland and the Chinese boy Ping. To all of these the house offers comfort, freedom, and adventure; the range of its sympathetic and inspiriting atmosphere extends far beyond its native family, far beyond England. It extends, in *The Chimneys of Green Knowe* and *The River at Green Knowe*, beyond ethnic boundaries; in Lucy Boston's masterpiece, *A Stranger at Green Knowe*, it finally extends beyond human boundaries too.

If the house is a still centre from which there emanate continuities of space in landscape, and receptiveness to people and creatures, so too it is a still centre in time, riding the centuries. The triumph of the books lies in their vivid, enlarging perspectives of space and time. As with the spatial adventure they offer, so the time sequence has nothing to do with the order of publi-cation of the books; nor is it equally important in them all; nor is it the province of any one child. *A Stranger at Green Knowe* is not concerned with time-perspectives at all; *The Stones of Green Knowe* is concerned with almost nothing else. In this, the most recently published of the series, an entirely new character makes his appearance: Roger d'Aulneaux, son of the house's founder. As he watches the walls raised, the windows placed, the first fire lit in the Knights' Hall, he is able with the aid of two magic stones to travel forward in time–forward to the time-points of other books, the seventeenth century of Toby, Alexander, and Linnet (*The Children of Green Knowe*), the eighteenth century of Susan and Jacob (*The Chimneys of Green Knowe*), and finally to the modern England of Tolly himself. As he moves forward he finds the house itself surviving to this day: 'Only the outside stairs were missing. It was worn and crumbly, weathered and gentle, like the two grand-mothers, but truly itself still. "O my house," he thought. "Live for ever"' (p 107). But the landscape near the house–his own densely forested landscape, wild with wolf and boar–has been cleared and domesticated down the cen-turies until in Tolly's England he finds a birdless and flowerless desolation, and asks himself, 'Could there have been a dreadful plague that had killed the lovely worldful?' It is in this novel that Mrs Boston's themes of change and changelessness achieve their clearest and most sombre focus: the best is that boy can still speak with boy across the centuries, the next best that the house, though crumbling and mortal like all things, is still there. But the landscape is a cry of defoliated pain.

Once Mrs Boston goes back further still–in *The River at Green Knowe*, when the children see antlered pagan dancers in the moonlight, long before the house was built. And in the story *The Guardians of the House* she seems to go speculatively beyond the present, to a time when the house is still further beleaguered by urban encroachment. In time as in space, the range and sensitivity of her imagination are moving and impressive. The fantasy of time-travel, the mystical, ghostly, affectionate communion of children across the centuries, is deftly reinforced by more tangible reminders of continuity and connection: family tradition means there is always a gardener called Boggis; the secret longevity of carp links past and present in the darkness of the moat; and when a small boy talks to his great-grandmother of her distant recollections, living memory is itself a marvel.

If continuity and change are Mrs Boston's most important theme, 'displacement' closely rivals it, associated as it is with her sense of the house as refuge and sanctuary for children and wild things. The theme of displacement is most prominent and varied in *The River at Green Knowe*, the only novel in the sequence which does not involve the Oldknow family. *The River at Green Knowe* is a curious book, episodic, patchy, and often contrived, its fantasy at times quite out of hand. It is by far the least successful of the *Green Knowe* books. Two 'displaced' boys, Oskar and Ping, share a boating and swimming holiday with the English girl Ida. Repeatedly the boys come up against images of their own displacement, and Oskar is quick to notice them. On the river they find a cygnet frantically trying to attach itself to foster-parents, and being driven off. It 'must be an orphan,' said Oskar. 'It's a Displaced Cygnet.' Later they discover the improbable figure of a former London bus driver, who has abandoned the rat-race for secret, isolated poverty in an unvisited backwater. Ping's first notion of this bizarre figure is that it's 'a he-witch' (witches are another of Lucy Boston's preoccupations). But Oskar knows otherwise: 'He's a displaced person that's escaped.' Later still they discover a displaced giant. And when they are carried back in time to the moonlit antlered dancers, it is Oskar who says, 'We are *really* displaced now.' No doubt Mrs Boston intends meaningful ironies, not least by this final comic understatement, but in practice the theme emerges as repetitive, contrived, and strident.

The River at Green Knowe also suffers from the lack of a 'grandmother'. Aged wisdom, in sympathetic collaboration with childhood–amused, discerning, and unfussed–is an essential element in the stories, and crucial to their vision and balance. In *The River at Green Knowe* it is missing, inadequately replaced by a couple of middle-aged eccentrics. One of these is a dotty archaeologist, concerned to prove the existence of prehistoric human giants. She is wildly excited when the children obligingly provide her with an authentic giant's tooth, but fails to persuade her scientific colleagues that it isn't faked. To the children she says, 'Ever heard the proverb, "There's none so blind as those that won't see"?' But when Terak the giant becomes a circus clown, and the children plot her final triumph by taking her to see him, it is she in her turn who 'won't see'. It can, she says, only be a fake and a contrivance, and Ping is left to reflect sadly on the perversity of grown-ups: 'I can't understand, when it's the thing they want most in the world, and it's there before their eyes, why they won't see it' (p 144).

The point is made, and the story spoilt. It has been manipulated, and its fantasy deprived of the credibility that fantasy demands, in order to enforce another (very Wordsworthian) theme that Mrs Boston holds precious–the vindication of childhood, its imaginative vision and sensuous energy and intellectual openness. This is a fundamental and moving theme in several of the stories, but in *The River at Green Knowe* it is too explicitly pursued, and made to issue in a false child-adult contrast.

Yet this same vision of childhood, and this same theme of displacement, are carried triumphantly forward into Mrs Boston's masterpiece, *A Stranger at Green Knowe*. By a happy decision she discarded the colourless Ida and the over-conscious Oskar, and chose to reintroduce the attractive, enigmatic Ping, uniting him in this novel not with benign eccentrics but with Mrs Oldknow herself. In the absence of Tolly, Ping is invited to Green Knowe for the holidays. Before his visit Ping has been with a school party to the zoo, and there become engrossed in sympathetic fascination with another 'displaced' creature like himself–the young gorilla Hanno.

Lucy Boston has written nothing finer than the opening section of this beautiful and tragic story, in which we are made to share, through a mar-vellous feat of creative imagination, the jungle childhood of Hanno, as he roves free with his family in the rank tropic vegetation of his steaming home-land. When he is caught and sent to an English zoo, we see through Ping's awareness the hideous confining concrete prison of his cage, and the scale of his massive frustrated strength. It is the beginning of an obsession in Ping, who has himself been displaced from jungle freedom to the demeaning concrete confines of a displaced person's camp, and the beginning of a strange and precarious comradeship between gorilla and boy. That Hanno, having escaped from the zoo, should find temporary refuge in the patch of undisturbed woodland at Green Knowe, is of course a hugely improbable coincidence, but Ping's obsessive care for the animal's movements makes it seem pre-ordained and inevitable. Hanno's freedom cannot last, of course, and the tragic outcome is also inevitable, but before that happens Hanno has enjoyed a respite of freedom worth a lifetime of captivity, and a relation-ship has formed between animal and boy which never seems anthropo-morphic or sentimental, but wholly convincing in its scrupulous fidelity to their separate forms of life. Unlike the other *Green Knowe* books, this is not a fantasy: it is both a moving, exciting story and a work of reverence for the wonder and uniqueness of the animal creation. We are made intimate with a life outside and beyond the human. If human beings are to make contact with it, as Ping does, the contact must be earned and suffered.

This sensuous understanding and care for the non-human is another of Lucy Boston's governing preoccupations. She has a remarkable capacity to tolerate, and even celebrate, the dispensability of man. Writing in her auto-biography about the genesis of *A Stranger at Green Knowe* she says: 'The subject to me was a big one. It had to contain the whole force of my belief that all life, not merely human, must have respect, that a man-centred con-ception of it was false and crippling, that these other lives are the great riches of ours. In particular I wanted to make clear my immense admiration for this creature so vulgarly shuddered at, and that there was no cosy answer to the wickedness that had been done to him' (*Memory in a House*, p 117).

The same idea recurs several times in *The Stones of Green Knowe*. Roger d'Aulneaux, guarding the sheep in a medieval sunrise, 'felt that he, a human, was the rare occasional creature, while the whole world teemed with millions of other species living out their different lives' (p 17), while Tolly, transported from our own times to Roger's darkening primeval forest, says, 'I shall be glad when we get out...Humans don't seem to be expected here, or wanted. It's almost as though they hadn't happened yet' (p 95).

Of all the many perspectives that Lucy Boston opens up for children in her stories, this is perhaps the widest and most challenging of all. From the still centre of Green Knowe, she moves with vision and intelligence through space and time, probing values, questioning 'progress', calling in doubt the self-conferred status of mankind.

Among these larger themes, the direct confrontation of good and evil is most explicit in *An Enemy at Green Knowe*, where the house is threatened by a modern witch, Dr Melanie D Powers, and defended against her by Grand-mother Oldknow, Tolly, and Ping. This book has attracted some adverse criticism, though of conflicting kinds. Some readers feel that overpowering evil is unconvincingly defeated by mere niceness and luck, others that the evil itself is unconvincing, since Dr Melanie Powers is not overpowering at all, but merely vindictive, pushing, and vulgar. Both criticisms seem to me to miss the point. There is indeed a potential evil in the house, to which Dr Melanie Powers seeks access, and it dates from the self-destructive witchcraft of a misguided seventeenth-century scholar. The supernatural attack is finally exorcised in the novel by a tremendous invocation of the powers of goodness. Yet evil has another, less terrifying but not for that reason less destructive face, and Dr Powers represents it. It is indeed stupid and vulgar, compounded of mindless egotism, superstition, and malice. It is insidious and relentless, and the more it is tolerated the more power it gains. This is the human and social evil, which in one form or another can abruptly enter people's lives, destroying established modes of living, interfering in hallowed privacies, poisoning security with doubt, wearing its vulgarian tenacity like armour. It is none the less evil because its manifestations are contemptible rather than awesome. But it too can be destroyed by the right adversary, using the right weapons: in this instance the successful chant of banishment is uttered by Tolly and Ping, and their weapons are not spiritual combat but mockery and laughter. What Lucy Boston convincingly shows in *An Enemy at Green Knowe* is not that evil can be vulgar, petty, and insensitive, but that vulgarity, insensitivity, and pettiness can be evil.

This is likewise the theme of her play, *The Horned Man*, which is also rooted in seventeenth-century witchcraft, and which shows what harm can overtake the innocent through mere superstition and malice, silliness and pride. In some respects it is also the theme of that first and remarkably distinguished novel *Yew Hall*, which was originally written for adults but has now reappeared in a series aimed at adolescent readers. (I suspect that only the most sophisticated adolescents will appreciate it, and that no one would have dreamed of finding it such a readership if Lucy Boston were not famous as a children's writer.) It is her first and most lyrical celebration of Hemingford Grey, and it is also a most subtle and claustrophobic thriller, lit with ironies and brilliantly constructed. It too shows how a seemingly trivial woman, silly, proud, and egotistical yet mindlessly determined, can cause an explosion of evil and tragedy. Arabella, in Lucy Boston's work, is an ancestor of Dr Melanie Powers.

There are other invigorating positives in Lucy Boston's work for children. Her feeling is strong and clear that children must be set free, to take their risks and grow: to climb the high trees, like Tolly and blind Susan in *The Chimneys of Green Knowe*, to swim the deep waters, like Jo and Toby in *The Sea Egg*. But perhaps the best of all her human images is Ping, who so delights Mrs Oldknow. He is the truly natural yet civilised child–contained, and polite within his oriental decorum, yet full of humour, zest, and enterprise, paddling his canoe 'with all the strength of his silky, melon–coloured back'.

In her cool, exact and graceful English, which like Ping himself combines a civilised decorum with sensuous joy, Lucy Boston communicates a unique and inspiriting vision. She is an uncompromising novelist; she makes no concessions; yet she is deservedly popular with a very wide age-range of readers. It is neither premature nor exaggerated to acknowledge her as a classic children's writer.

(1976)

Books by L M Boston

Yew Hall Faber, 1954, re-issued Bodley Head, Books for New Adults, 1972
The Children of Green Knowe Faber, 1954
The Chimneys of Green Knowe Faber, 1958
The River at Green Knowe Faber, 1959
A Stranger at Green Knowe Faber, 1961
An Enemy at Green Knowe Faber, 1964 (Carnegie Medal)
The Castle of Yew Bodley Head, 1965
The Sea Egg Faber, 1967
The House that Grew Faber, 1969
The Horned Man (a play for children) Faber, 1970
Nothing Said Faber, 1971
Memory in a House (an autobiography) Bodley Head, 1973
The Guardians of the House Bodley Head, 1974
The Fossil Snake Bodley Head, 1975
The Stones of Green Knowe Bodley Head, 1976

Leon Garfield

by

RHODRI JONES

LEON GARFIELD dislikes being described as a writer for children. He regards this as a publisher's convenience–a slot into which his books can be easily put. What interests him is the novel as narrative, and since the modern novel for adults tends to be concerned with psychological states and sexual exploration rather than with the telling of an intricate and neatly dove-tailing story, Garfield's novels are regarded as being more suitable for children. Certainly they appeal very strongly to young readers and a very important element of this appeal is the strong story-line.

Each of his novels is built on a complicated but firm plot, following the adventures of the main character through a series of clues and discoveries until the complications are resolved and the mysteries revealed as the novel comes to a close. The plots are usually based on a search of some kind–in *Jack Holborn* and *Devil-in-the-Fog* for the truth about the hero's origin, in *The Drummer Boy* for what is real and what is false. Always there is the search for knowledge.

Another factor which gives the novels an appeal for young people is the type of hero that Garfield depicts. Garfield's heroes are on their own. They have to make their own way in the bewildering adult world, finding out for themselves what is reality and what is illusion, learning by trial and error whom to trust and who is merely making use of them. There is Smith, for instance, the twelve-year-old pickpocket stealing a living in fog-swirled eighteenth-century London, who learns that mere survival is not enough and that compassion is more important than wounded pride or self-interest. Or Charlie Samson, the golden drummer boy, whose goodness is taken advantage of and who learns that the adult world of pride and privilege is not all that it seems. It is through heroes like these that children can explore the strange adult world into which they are moving and against whom they can weigh their own experience.

The style Garfield uses also appeals to children. His language is highly coloured, full of imagery and humour, shot through with irony and ambiguity (which last may not always be grasped by children). Sometimes the imagery is used decoratively (the monkey 'stared out at the passing world with eyes like undertaker's buttons'; she laughed 'a merry tinkling sound, like a dish full of shillings'–from *The Boy and the Monkey*); often, it is used more organically as part of the meaning of the novel. In *Smith*, the dead eyes of the magistrate are a symbol of his inward blindness. In *The Drummer Boy*, the golden lad is in danger of having his innocence tarnished by the world.

Even in the most grim situation–for Garfield shuns little from murder to madness–humour keeps breaking through. Jack Holborn, becalmed on an equatorial sea, says, 'If Hell is as hot as that terrible morning, then I'm not going there!' The opening of *Smith* gives another good example of this:

He was called Smith and was twelve years old. Which, in itself, was a miracle; for it seemed as if the smallpox, the consumption, brain-fever, gaol-fever and even the hangman's rope had given him a wide berth for fear of catching something. Or else they weren't quick enough.

The opening of *Smith* illustrates also the assurance with which Garfield establishes a style and a tone for his novels, a skill he may have learned from Jane Austen who has certainly influenced his use of irony, the flavour of which can again be best shown by quotation, this time from *Black Jack*:

Here Mrs Mitchell knew what she was talking about. She'd a great long experience of not knowing. Close on thirty years of it. In her competent, assured way, she was something of an expert in ignorance...

Another example is this comment by Dr Jones and Parson Hall, owners of a swindling asylum, on the blackmailing Hatch: 'Pray to God he knew no more than he'd said. For the conduct of their establishment was no more above reproach than anything mortal.' It is not surprising that when asked to contribute his choice to an anthology of writing for children, Garfield should have chosen Jane Austen's *History of England*.

The other main influence on Garfield's writing seems to be Dickens, although he did not read Dickens until after he had written his first novel *Jack Holborn*. This can be seen partly in the characterisation of the minor figures with their one easily recognisable catch-phrase or trait (Meg in *Smith* with her 'Learning? Give you a farthing for it!' or Pobjoy in *Jack Holborn* with his thirst for gin). It can be seen partly in the gusto and skill of the narrative. The whirling end of *Black Jack* is like a speeded-up version of the crescendo of crisis upon crisis at the end of *A Tale of Two Cities* or *Oliver Twist*. It can be seen partly in the use of symbolism. The travelling actors of *Devil-in-the-Fog* and the fair people of *Black Jack* with their casual, free-and-easy emotional world bear the same significance as the circus people in *Hard Times*. It can be seen in the way in which, once he gets going, Garfield's prose takes on a lyrical lilt and rhythm reminiscent of Dickens in full flight:

Books in their fluttering and dusty thousands poured and thumped down as if the very skies had been loaded with them. Histories, Memoirs, Diaries, Lexicons, Grammars, Atlases, Journals, Biographies, Poems, Plays...books about heaven, books about hell, huge books about pygmies, tiny books about giants–even books about books–all, all slid and tumbled into a desperate ruin overhung by a bitter cloud of dust. And some-where underneath it all, still jerking and twitching, though feebly now, lay the unlucky bookseller himself!

It is this kind of exuberant exaggeration and vitality in the use of words that Garfield shares with Dickens. He also shares a warmth of heart and feeling. Virtue is triumphant. Goodness is seen to be good, without in any way descending to Dickens' sentimental excesses. This is not to say that Garfield is a greater artist than Dickens–merely that he has a better sense of proportion.

Garfield's novels are set in the eighteenth century. He has said (in an inter-view in *The Guardian*, 9 June 1971): 'It's like science fiction in reverse: you take a moral problem out of context to observe it better; you have the reality of the past to latch on to.' Through the vividness of his writing, his choice of detail and the generosity of his characterisation, Garfield does bring a past age to life. *Smith* has the exuberance, the violence, the high spirits, and the squalor of *The Beggar's Opera*. But his novels are more than costume charades. Moral questions and their reverberations loom very large. The search for identity is made concrete by having his hero literally search to find out who his father is in *Jack Holborn* and *Devil-in-the-Fog*. Moral choice is a very important element in *Smith*. Learning to distinguish between outward beauty, respect-ability or rank and inward corruption, self-seeking, and wickedness is the basis of *Black Jack* and *The Drummer Boy*. Even in as slight a tale as *The Boy and the Monkey*, the value of a human life in terms of cash is considered.

And this is, perhaps, one of the most important aspects of Garfield's novels. They deal with the same kind of themes as adult literature, but in terms that children can understand. By identifying with the heroes, children can appre-ciate the moral choices that arise, and can see that the world is not entirely black and white but varying shades of grey. When they go on to read Shakespeare, Dickens, George Eliot or Jane Austen, they are prepared for similar complexities of feelings and responses to character and situation. If they do not go on to read these classics, they have had a valuable and easily approachable substitute.

Garfield's first novel, *Jack Holborn*, has a touch of Stevenson about its subject-matter. It is a fantastic fast-moving story taking in all the clichés of boys' adventure stories–a foundling uncluttered by parents, stowing away, capture by pirates, attempted mutiny, confusion between two identical brothers, shipwreck, a treasure chest, an unlucky diamond, slave trading. Coincidence stalks the plot. Yet this paraphernalia of adventure is only superficial and underneath it lie philosophical questions that have a reality. Already, Garfield has established the main themes of his writing. Jack is a foundling who is trying to make his way in the world and trying to find out who his mother is–and therefore who *he* is. The differences between appearance and reality are brought out in the confusion between the two brothers, one a pirate captain who manages to trick his hanging judge brother into changing places. The theme reaches its climax in the courtroom as the judge is on trial for piracy and murder and is being tried by his pirate brother. Which is the judge? Which is the pirate? How can one tell by looking?

The other main theme is Jack's search for true values, for integrity, truth, the difference between good and evil. When Jack first meets the villainous captain, he hero-worships him and sees him as a fallen angel. It is not until the end, when Jack sees the captain tormenting the last hours of a condemned man, that he really sees through the external charm and glamour and realises how he is being used.

Devil-in-the-Fog explores the theme of identity in greater depth. George, brought up as son of the itinerant acting and conjuring Treet family, finds that he is the long-lost son of a country baronet. He has to make an adjustment between his exhibitionist extrovert nature and the reserve required of an English gentleman. But then he discovers that it was all a trick. Mr Treet is his real father after all and has 'sold' him. In the end he returns to the Treet troupe. It is a more straightforward story than *Jack Holborn*, more compactly centred on the two family backgrounds. A contrast is built up between the two worlds–the Treets casual, familiar, proud, and emotional with Mr Treet like Mr Micawber, benevolent and ineffectual; the Dexters reserved, cold, not showing emotion or showing off. And in the centre is George, not knowing which world he belongs to, trying to find out the truth. Perhaps the dénouement is too hurried and the inevitable conflict of loyalties within George not fully enough explored or resolved. And the translation of Lady Dexter, herself a haunting figure, enigmatic, ironic, strangely attractive, into the London benefactress of the Treets is rather glib, but the reader rejoices that her hidden feelings emerge triumphantly in the end and that she is able to break way from the cold reserve of her class.

With *Smith*, Garfield moves confidently into his stride. The plot is in-geniously worked, revolving round Smith's theft of a document from a man who is subsequently murdered. The events are misted by irony and ambi-guity. Smith's treasure trove, the document, is useless to him because he can't read. He makes a friend–but he is blind. The bland, smiling Mr Billing is a villain. Lord Tom, the glorious highwayman, is a coward and a traitor. Mr Mansfield is as blind as the Blind Lady he serves.

The theme of reality and illusion is continued. Smith learns that his hero,

'the glittering, dangerous highwayman', has betrayed him. The scales fall
from his eyes and he sees Lord Tom for what he is, a shabby, seedy double-
dealer. But that is not the whole story, because Lord Tom redeems himself
by saving Smith at the cost of his own life. Perhaps Smith's hero-worship
was not misplaced after all, for Lord Tom 'went like the grandest toby of
them all'. Smith also makes strides in maturity. Although abandoned by the
magistrate on suspicion of murder, Smith saves his life and shows more trust
in humanity than the magistrate has been capable of doing. He comes to
realise that 'nothing holds him but affection, and nothing feeds this affection
so much as the deep understanding of his own fair situation in his blind
friend's dark world'. Mr Mansfield also undertakes 'a very strange journey-
from justice to compassion'. About them all swirls the fervid life of London,
full of cut-throats and highwaymen, the busy traffic of the streets and passage-
ways, the world of dubious taverns and sordid prisons, the fogs, the stench,
the gin. Out of this muck-heap Smith blossoms, Mr Mansfield's guardian
angel, 'a little singed and tattered about the wings–but then he's flown
through the caves of hell!' It is a rich story of a hard, quick, determined
London lad making his way among the moral quicksands of growing up
and making good that should appeal to any young reader.

The hero of *Black Jack* is not made of such stern stuff–at least on the
surface–but he also makes it. Tolly Dorking is insecure and uncertain. First
shackled to a giant ruffian who has escaped hanging, and then to Belle, an
escaped lunatic, he manages by sticking strongly to his own principles to
influence both for the better. In this way, he is able to find himself and reach
maturity, whereby he shakes off his sense of inferiority before his largely
unseen sea captain uncle and finds him comic, not frightening, when they
are reunited at the end. As in *Devil-in-the-Fog*, there is a contrast between
various worlds–the respectable world of Captain Dorking, the free and precarious world of the travelling fair, the outwardly respectable but inwardly
hypocritical world of the Reigate Carters, the corrupt world of Dr Jones,
Parson Hall, Hatch, and the Islington madhouse, and of Mrs Gorgandy and
her selling of corpses. The novel builds up to a tremendous climax as the
race to save Belle from the madhouse and reach the safety of Captain Dorking's ship is mingled with the warnings, hysteria, and panic of the London
earthquake scare of 1750. The themes treated are possibly more adult–the
theme of madness, the love of Tolly for Belle–but essentially the novel is
again the search of adolescence for its own identity and confidence in itself
in a shifting adult world. Throughout, the image of the sea and a journey
home is seen as the searching and resolution of Tolly's own journey to find
himself. It is a hard and cruel world that Tolly has to struggle against. Of
his enemy Hatch (a kind of Artful Dodger, but not so endearing), Parson
Hall says, 'Believe you me, Almighty God was angry when he fashioned

that one out of dust–He never *breathed* into him–He roundly *spat!*' Yet young readers can take some assurance from the fact that Tolly–gentle, unsure, sensitive–did come through. I feel that *Black Jack* is perhaps Garfield's supreme achievement.

The three stories in *Mister Corbett's Ghost* are slighter but show similar preoccupations. In the title story, an apprentice, Benjamin Partridge, through a pact with a devilish old man, kills his hateful master, but then finds himself taking pity on his master's ghost, and all is restored as it was. Benjamin has matured, come to terms with experience and realised that all is not what it seems and that sympathy on his part is needed to understand the adult world. In *Vaarlam and Tripp*, another rather snobbish apprentice comes to appreciate the skill of his master, an artist, who had at first seemed merely vulgar, dirty, and cowardly. In *The Simpleton*, Nick is manoeuvred through his innocence and love for one of the passengers into being the excuse for Mr Bartleman, an embezzler of souls as well as of money, to try to take over the ship. Nick finds the courage and resourcefulness to defeat him through his love for Caroline. As the author says, 'For where else can lie the strength of the gentle and the meek save in love?' It is a powerful story of evil attempting to use good for its foul ends and failing.

This can also be seen as the main theme of *The Drummer Boy*. It is a story of disillusionment, of innocence in danger of being corrupted and dragged down by the greed and self-interest of the world. The hero, Charlie Samson, is used by the other characters. They seek assurance in his golden youthful radiance. Mr Shaw, the disreputable surgeon, wants to use Charlie as his entré into society. Sophia wants to use him to deliver her father, the General, from the danger of a court-martial. Charlie has fallen in love with Sophia and is prepared to perjure himself for her sake to save her father. But through-out the novel runs the image of what happens to golden drummer boys when they become old and tarnished by the world. Charlie is haunted by the sight of a beggar and sees what he might become: 'And for the first time it racked his heart that he might tarnish and wrinkle and hobble by the wayside…and come to beg in Wardour Street.' It is through Mr Shaw that Charlie sees what kind of people the General and Sophia are: 'The father feeds her–and she feeds him. She feeds him on vanity; and he feeds her on death, endless death, endless death–.' Charlie breaks away from Sophia and finds safety in the genuine love of Charity, Sophia's maid, and returns to the simple way of life of his fathers.

As often in Garfield's novels (Solomon Trumpet in *Jack Holborn*, Lord Tom in *Smith*), it is a secondary character who helps the hero to see his way more clearly. Mr Shaw's love for Charlie is doomed. He tries to cling to money and success, but his love for Charlie is greater than his material self-interest, and his is the voice of reality that awakens Charlie from his dreams of illusion, though it means that Mr Shaw's own hopes are dashed for ever. But through this action Mr Shaw is also himself redeemed.

The Drummer Boy ranges from the glory of the battlefield transformed into horror, perhaps symbolised by Mr Shaw collecting teeth from the dead to sell to the toothless back home, through the grim comedy of Corporal Finch trying out his new teeth which make his speech unintelligible ('Splendid as they were, Corporal Finch's fine French teeth had stretched his lines of communication till they'd all but snapped') to the simple sweetness and goodness of Charity when Charlie makes up his mind to believe Mr Shaw and abandon Sophia. The author's sole comment is, 'Charity's eyes were gleaming like stars.' Garfield shows that growing up is hard, but with determination you can win through.

(1972)

Postscript

Leon Garfield's five early novels–*Jack Holborn, Devil-in-the-Fog, Smith, Black Jack*, and *The Drummer Boy*–established very clearly the kind of world we associate with Garfield's writing. Since then, he has continued to produce prolifically, but the sense of unity, the sense of direction, seems to have become dissipated. It is not just a question of wanting or expecting him to go on writing as he has done or to write about the same things as before. After all, one doesn't expect each of William Mayne's books, for example, to be the same–in fact, one is surprised and gratified that each new novel is different and unpredictable. Nor does Garfield's later work lack quality–*The God Beneath the Sea, The Strange Affair of Adelaide Harris*, and *The Ghost Downstairs* are as fine as anything he has written. But nevertheless, looking back at the work he has produced since *The Drummer Boy*, there is a slight nagging sense of disappointment as though Garfield has missed his footing or somehow stumbled from the path and only intermittently found it again. He seems to be turning round seeking new directions, not all of which lead to successful destinations.

The quintessential Garfield world of the early novels is most instantly recognisable in his subsequent short novels. Stories like *The Boy and the Monkey, The Captain's Watch*, and *Lucifer Wilkins* show the characteristic delight of playing with words and images and the creation of chirpy characters. The more recent *Mirror, Mirror* and *The Lamplighter's Funeral*, two of a projected twelve under the general heading of 'Garfield's Apprentices', mark a very definite return to the London of narrow streets and evocative names, of master craftsmen and beggared children–though perhaps the squalor is more readily revealed. As though to symbolise this, the lamplighter's apprentice goes out of his way to illuminate gin-sodden women collapsed in alleyways and furtive lovers on doorsteps.

Another element which has previously been evident in Garfield's writing–though not, strangely, in the major novels–is an interest in the supernatural, but none of his ghost stories has been as extended and successful as *The Ghost Downstairs*. It is innovatory in that it is set outside the eighteenth century, in the time of children's sailor suits, of cabs and trains. Mr Fast, a dried-up legal clerk, thinks he has tricked Mr Fishbane, an eccentric embodiment of the devil. He has given him seven years off his life in return for riches–but off the beginning of his life, not the end. It is only when the ghost of the seven-year-old child Mr Fast once was appears that the clerk's terrors begin. The story is told with grim power though not without the touches of irony and humour that are characteristic.

Comedy is always bursting out in Garfield's work, but with *The Strange Affair of Adelaide Harris* comedy has taken over completely. The story has the riotous to-ing and fro-ing of a farce by Feydeau. The characters are all swept along in a fantastic dance as complication upon complication is piled up to a masterly dénouement. Every detail is right; every incident builds up our knowledge of the characters and tangles or untangles the skein of the plot more. No word is wasted. It is a virtuoso performance, whose virtuosity can be gauged by comparing it with the short story *The Restless Ghost*, where the two schoolboy heroes, Bostock and Harris, who set the dance going by exposing the infant Adelaide on the hillside in emulation of Ancient Sparta, made an earlier appearance. In the short story, Bostock and Harris are merely rather mischievous schoolboys involved in a prank that becomes too big for them. In *The Strange Affair of Adelaide Harris* they have been purified and refined; they have come into focus. Harris is the one with the cunning brain and the deep thought, Bostock his more sensitive but rather dense friend (except that it is Bostock who shows the real intelligence) with an undying admiration for and devotion to his supposed genius of a hero. They are not just schoolboys, they are quintessential schoolboys. No wonder Mr Brett, their history tutor, looks at them with dread.

The atmosphere of this comedy is more Regency than eighteenth century, which is appropriate since the novel is set in Brighton, and perhaps the change of scene from murky London is responsible for the lightness of touch and the hilarity of the proceedings. Certainly, Garfield's new venture of writing a comic novel is a total success.

Another direction Garfield was moving in was towards collaboration. *The Ghost Downstairs*, for instance, could almost be described as a joint work with the illustrator, Antony Maitland. But the most important collaboration has been with Edward Blishen in their retelling of the Greek myths in *The God Beneath the Sea* and *The Golden Shadow*, where the myths are given a fresh power and a new and strong narrative unity. The strength of these two books lies in the sweep of the story-telling and in the austere nobility of the tone, which except in occasional ironic asides is strangely unlike the Garfield of the earlier novels and shows a greater restraint. The characters come alive without losing dignity. The stories are filled in with details that convince–the hawkers selling purses of sand stained with the blood of the Nemean Lion in the market place of Mycenae, for example–so that a sense of bustling life is given to this strange mixture of heroic endeavour, godly power and human frailty without in any way diminishing the grandeur and awesomeness of the events. Both volumes (*The Golden Shadow* marginally less so) are splendid achievements, and rescue the myths from past flat and fustian versions–even if one may sometimes have to go back to those versions to find out what the myths actually and factually were.

It is with the three major novels that Garfield has written since *The Drummer Boy* that doubts really begin to press. *The Sound of Coaches* has a theme reminiscent of the earlier *Jack Holborn* and *Devil-in-the-Fog* with its hero Sam searching for his real father and finding disillusionment along the way. The world of the coaching trade and the travelling actors that Sam joins are vividly portrayed, but somehow Sam is too pale a character for us to care very much about him. *The Prisoners of September* deals with the involvement of two young Englishmen in the massacres of September 1793 in Paris. They are like two halves of the same character, one glorying in the brutality while believing himself to be fighting for freedom, the other repelled by the horror of it. Unthinking idealism takes a hard knock. *The Pleasure Garden* is set in a kind of open-air brothel, based presumably on Vauxhall Gardens, where children hide all night in the trees and report on the goings-on for the purpose of blackmail.

It is not simply that these novels display an increasing though only occasional coarseness of language and violence. There is the cellarman Joe in *The Sound of Coaches,* for instance, talking about the sun 'shining out of the tiddler's arse'; there is Richard Mortimer in *The Prisoners of September* inciting the crowd to tear a young woman's body to pieces and the vision of packs of wild dogs rushing through the streets of Paris with the private parts of princesses in their jaws; there is the whole idea of children being involved in voyeurism and blackmail in *The Pleasure Garden*. These were crude and violent times, and foul language can be justified in terms of character, but are such things suitable reading for children?

Garfield has always resented being regarded as a children's writer, and there have been violent and unpleasant episodes in his earlier novels, but the subject-matter of his recent novels seems more suitable for adults than for children. They raise the question of what is a children's writer, which is a large topic but a part of whose answer is to do with tone, the way the author addresses his imagined audience. And while Garfield is writing about things which more suitably concern adults than children, his tone is still that which one would use when talking to children alone, with the result that the end-product is satisfactory neither to one nor to the other. Alan Garner in *The Red Shift* appears to be concerned with his own ingenuity and doesn't care who he is writing for. Stephanie Plowman in *Three Lives for the Czar* seems to be writing for adults, although her novels happen to have been published for 'Young People'. Garfield is in between. He wants to communicate, and he wants to communicate to children and adults, but this is only possible in exceptional circumstances–and usually long after the author is dead. It seems appropriate that the figure of Prometheus should loom so large in *The God Beneath the Sea.*

RHODRI JONES

Books by Leon Garfield

Fiction

Jack Holborn Longman, 1964
Devil-in-the-Fog Longman, 1966
Smith Longman, 1967
Black Jack Longman, 1968
The Boy and the Monkey Heinemann, 1969
The Drummer Boy Longman, 1970
The God Beneath the Sea (with Edward Blishen) Longman, 1970
The Strange Affair of Adelaide Harris Longman, 1971
The Captain's Watch Heinemann, 1972
The Ghost Downstairs Longman, 1972
Lucifer Wilkins Heinemann, 1973
The Golden Shadow (with Edward Blishen) Longman, 1973 (Carnegie Medal)
The Sound of Coaches Kestrel Books, 1974
The Prisoners of September Kestrel Books, 1975
The Lamplighter's Funeral, Garfield's *Apprentices* Series, Heinemann, 1976
Mirror, Mirror, Garfield's *Apprentices* Series, Heinemann, 1976
The Pleasure Garden Kestrel Books, 1976

Collections

Mister Corbett's Ghost and Other Stories Longman, 1969
The Restless Ghost: Three Stories Pantheon, New York, 1969
Baker's Dozen edited by Leon Garfield, Ward Lock, 1973
Kaleidoscope edited by Leon Garfield, Purnell, 1973
Adventures of the Boy and the Monkey (comprising *The Boy and the Monkey*, *The Captain's Watch*, and *Lucifer Wilkins*) Puffin, 1976

Non-Fiction

Child O' War (with David Proctor) Collins, 1972
The House of Hanover André Deutsch, 1976

Alan Garner

by

TONY WATKINS

'*Myth is not entertainment, but rather the crystallisation of experience, and far from being escapist literature, fantasy is an intensification of reality.*' Alan Garner.

'*Like poetry, fantasy uses a metaphorical approach to the perception of universal truth.*' Lilian H Smith, *The Unreluctant Years—a critical approach to children's literature.*

ALAN GARNER's four novels find the source of their inspiration in non-classical mythology and all contain elements of fantasy. The importance of myths for children is now generally accepted. Norse and Celtic myths in particular contain the roots of our culture–roots that affect both the social and personal lives of our children, who possess the past within them. By their freshness and strange vivid beauty the stories appeal to minds full of wonder at the nature of things. For the 'old tales are deeply concerned with ...early fantasies, feelings, needs, and motives of behaviour, which they incorporate for us in story form' (Joan E Cass, *Literature and the Young Child*, Longmans, 1967, p 28).

For Alan Garner there are no original stories: 'originality now means the personal colouring of existing themes, and some of the richest ever expressed are in the folklore of Britain.' (Note to *The Moon of Gomrath*.) For example, *Elidor* combines the story of Childe Roland with, among other things, the Irish myth of the Tuatha Dé Danaan who came from the 'southern isles of the world'. The four treasures of Elidor closely resemble Nuada's sword, Lugh's lance, Dagda's cauldron, and the Stone of Fal which they brought with them to Ireland. But Alan Garner takes these elements of myth and folklore and skilfully transmutes them, in an almost poetic way, into new metaphors of experience. By this process the half-forgotten stories and beliefs acquire a powerful, living reality, making their presence felt in the lives of the children of our complex, mechanistic, industrial society.

In a *Times Literary Supplement* article ('A Bit More Practice', 6 June 1968), Alan Garner explained that he writes for adolescents: 'by adolescence I mean an arbitrary age from, say, ten to eighteen'. This attempt to write for the difficult, transitional period between childhood and adulthood means that his novels need to satisfy at various levels: at the simple, narrative level of suspense and what happens next, through the deeper levels of characterisation, to adult concerns of symbol and theme. In this, it seems to me, the later novels have been particularly successful.

The first of the four novels, *The Weirdstone of Brisingamen*, although weak in places, brings alive the world of magic in its eternal cosmic fight of the forces of good against the forces of evil. To Alan Garner this world of magic lies close to the surface of our world and at times forces us to recognise its existence. Thus Colin and Susan find themselves involved in protecting Firefrost (the weirdstone of Freyja's necklace, Brisingamen) against the powers of darkness who can destroy the world as we know it. The book has a particularly strong impact upon children of nine to thirteen, the children of the middle schools. One instance of this is related by Gordon H Mould in an article in *The School Librarian*, Vol 15, No 2, July 1967.

In *The Weirdstone* we see the beginnings of a theme running throughout the novels: the magic of the old myths exerts a profound effect upon the present. Through this influence ordinary everyday objects become charged with magical and mythological significance and seemingly ordinary people become involved in the conflict that takes place on a universal scale. One experiences a fine *frisson* of terror as one realises that the innocuous-looking hikers are in reality the agents of darkness. Again in *Elidor* a piece of iron railing, a broken cup, a stone, and a wooden sword are charged with energy that originates in the other world; and in *The Owl Service* a patterned dinner service holds within itself powerful forces which threaten to destroy relationships.

In *The Weirdstone* Colin and Susan are rather flat, insignificant characters, but in *The Moon of Gomrath* they are more fully realised, with Susan in particular exemplifying some of Alan Garner's later powers of characterisation. Like Helen and Alison in the later books, it is through Susan that the magical forces work. It is she who releases the Old Magic from its sleep: 'it is magic of the heart, not of the head: it can be felt but not known' (p 76, Penguin edition). The magical forces, which one feels are so external in *The Weirdstone*, are here partially identified with the forces arising within Susan herself as she grows from childhood to womanhood. She begins her ride with the Wild Hunt but is compelled to break off, for she is 'but green in power'; the forces within her do not as yet attain fulfilment.

The Moon of Gomrath develops another important theme running through all the novels: modern industrialised Britain has forgotten and is even destroying her mythological past; society is thus cutting itself off from its roots. The lios-alfar (the elves of light) are dying from the smoke-sickness of a polluted England, and the other creatures of folklore have withdrawn from men's eyes. Cadellin tells Susan:

'It has not always been so. Once we were close; but some little time before the elves were driven away, a change came over you. You found the world easier to master by hands alone; things became more than thoughts with you, and you called it an Age of Reason . . . For these reasons we withdrew from mankind, and became a memory, and with the years, a superstition, ghosts and terrors for a winter's night; and later a mockery and a disbelief.'

In *Elidor* the forces of the other world reassert themselves and 'break through' to disrupt the comfortable middle-class existence of the Watson family. Washing machine, television, and food-mixer go berserk under the influence of the power pouring from the four treasures of Elidor; and it is in a partially completed new housing estate that Findhorn the unicorn bursts through from the other world. In *The Owl Service* the force of myth has become so powerful that it almost controls the thoughts and actions of the characters, compelling them to act out the old Welsh legend once again.

The Owl Service (awarded the Carnegie Medal for 1967) is at once Alan Garner's finest and most complex work to date. It is a novel for older children and adults, and part of its value for the upper forms of the secondary school lies in the fact that adolescents can here find the theme of love and jealousy treated in a sensitive and mature way (although the word 'love' is nowhere mentioned in the relationship between Alison, Roger, and Gwyn). The setting of the story is the Welsh valley where centuries ago was enacted the tragedy of Lleu Llaw Gyffes, his wife Blodeuwedd, and her lover Gronw Pebyr, one of the lords of darkness. (The original legend is to be found in the Fourth Branch of the Mabinogion: 'Math, son of Mathonwy'.) Through the influence of some strange power that seems to derive ultimately from the earth itself–perhaps from the flowers from which Blodeuwedd was created as a wife for Lleu–generation after generation of the inhabitants of the valley have been compelled to re-enact the story in their own lives. Yet the power is at the same time reinforced and modified by the passions of the characters through whom it works. As with Susan in *The Moon of Gomrath*, there is no clear division between the forces without and the forces within. In the generation before the three children, Huw's wife Nancy found a lover in Bertram. The forces within (call them psychic forces, if you will), reinforced by the power from without, turned destructive, the owls went hunting, and Huw caused Bertram's death.

Gwyn (Huw's son by Nancy) inherits the 'lordship' of the valley, but now the roles are changed. In the sparse, economical style of the novel not a word is wasted and even the names of the characters are significant; Roger (meaning 'fame-spear'), like Lleu, has to contend with 'one of the lords of darkness' (Gwynn was the Welsh god of the underworld) for Alison. Again the forces turn destructive and the owls go hunting. In the superb climax to the novel,

Roger resists the revenging dark feelings within him, and by his act of forgiveness the owls are transformed into flowers.

Interwoven into this central theme are other themes: the challenge of an intelligent and vital working-class boy to the accepted and somewhat effete middle-class conventions and proprieties; and the humiliating, potentially explosive situation whereby the Welsh cannot afford to keep their own houses and lands but must sell out to the English. At the end of the novel, however, there is the suggestion of resolution, of a possible synthesis of opposites that lies somewhere in the future. It is sufficient to say that *The Owl Service* is a sensitive and powerful novel that repays several re-readings.

It was C S Lewis who said: 'No book is really worth reading at the age of ten which is not equally (and often far more) worth reading at the age of fifty...'; I think he would have been more than pleased with Alan Garner's four novels.

(1969)

Postscript on 'Red Shift'

In *Red Shift* (1973), pattern is all-important. The prose is lean and meaning elusive: the outline of patterns delicately traced (as in the axehead that links the levels of the story) is what remains in the mind after reading the novel, together with many questions and puzzles. Time past and time present mingle, resonate, and finally coalesce. As in the previous books, the past is never lost: it may be overlaid perhaps, but, looking carefully, one can still distinguish the old lines, the old tracks, and here they lead to the sacred places, the centres of energy at which people worship: sacred mound and church stand close by one another in *Red Shift*.

The forces at work are transmuted and realised in different forms in the three strands of time: in each, a young man and young woman attempt to shape a loving relationship in a world of violent destructiveness. Tom, Thomas, and Macey are aspects of one another: each of them sees beyond the normal bounds of vision and the results are powerfully disturbing. Each handles the votive axehead, a talisman that is handed through time and finally tamed when Tom sells it to the British Museum. The time strands are not linear but offer dimensions of the same concerns: Tom uses phrases from Plautus, the Roman soldiers speak like American GIs; we see the light from Orion, the hunter, which started on its way when the Romans occupied England.

The meaning is oblique, ambiguous, at times infuriatingly tantalising. It seems to lie partly within the geometry of relationships in the book: *between* the triangles set up by characters, places, times. It is implied, hinted at, rather than stated. All this makes the novel difficult to write about explicitly. But the same concerns are as in the earlier books—it is as if Alan Garner were working and reworking the seams of a landscape and the result is a novel whose texture is as uncompromising as millstone grit.

TONY WATKINS

Books by Alan Garner

The Weirdstone of Brisingamen Collins, 1960
The Moon of Gomrath Collins, 1963
Elidor Collins, 1965
Holly for the Bongs; a Nativity Play (with Roger Hill) Collins, 1967
The Old Man of Mow (with Roger Hill) Collins, 1967
The Owl Service Collins, 1967 (Carnegie Medal)
Red Shift Collins, 1973
The Bread Horse Collins, 1975
The Stone Book Collins, 1976

Anthologies

The Book of Goblins Hamish Hamilton, 1969
The Guizer: a Book of Fools Hamish Hamilton, 1975

Cynthia Harnett

by

WINIFRED WHITEHEAD

CYNTHIA HARNETT has written some half-dozen historical stories for children. Four of these now form a quartet, covering between them a continuous period of about eighty years, from 1415 to 1493. These years, historically speaking, span the troubled times from the Battle of Agincourt under Henry V through the Wars of the Roses to the time when Henry Tudor was firmly established on the throne. During this period both England's foreign pretensions in France and internal dissensions over the succession to the throne were painfully resolved, and during this period too the years conveniently marked off as the Middle Ages had largely come to an end and a new era in Europe had begun. But it would be a mistake to think that these four books attempt in any real sense to interpret the political or cultural progress of these years. The advent of the printing press under Caxton is indeed the central event of one book, *The Load of Unicorn*, but its effects are seen only as they concern one family of scriveners. Political events are the background to underground plotting in this book and in several of the others, but here too they arouse interest only as they affect the individuals concerned, and for the most part the involvement of the central characters is involuntary, almost accidental. Certainly none of the heroes, or their families, ever seriously challenge the existing order. Their loyalty to the established regime is taken for granted–even Matthew and Cornelius, Bendy's unpleasant stepbrothers, are horror-stricken to discover that their meanness has led them unwittingly to finance the plots of Henry Tudor's followers. 'We had no thought of treason,' cried Cornelius shakily. 'How could we know about Lancastrian plottings?' And though their shakiness and unwillingness to be involved are dictated entirely by concern for their own necks, the prevailing tone of the book suggests that conscious treachery is even more unthinkable than the small-minded self-interest and resistance to change which led them to this plight. That 'good' must mean also 'loyal to the reigning King' is seen clearly in the next volume, *The Woolpack*, for here the reigning king is the very Henry Tudor whose followers were traitors in the preceding story, and the troubled years in between are dismissed lightly enough. 'But it was nearly eight years since the Battle of Bosworth Field, where King Richard the Third had been killed, and King Henry Tudor had put on the crown, and nowadays everything was peaceful.'

So there is no deep questioning of events and loyalties in Cynthia Harnett's books. Kings may come and kings may go, religious faiths may change, as in *Stars of Fortune* under Mary Tudor, but these great events exist only on the edge of the lives of her heroes, who follow their ordinary domestic concerns comparatively unruffled by political change.

This approach has its justification. For the ordinary citizen, from the country-bred lad to the city scrivener or prosperous wool merchant, the chief aim in life was to live quietly, maintaining as well as he might the security, well-being, and honour of his own family and friends, whoever might be the power behind the throne. And, more important to this writer, such an approach leaves her free to concentrate on what is the greatest concern and indeed the main strength of her books, the patient, loving exposition of the details of the everyday life of the time. In each book she describes with infinite care and skill the daily life of her young hero, his place within his society, his family relationships and his initiation into young adulthood with all the difficulties and adjustments this may bring. All the material aspects of his life are documented; details of the streets and wharves of London, the construction and furnishing of houses, the work and play of the young adolescent at home, at school, as apprentice or merchant's son, in London or in country town or village.

Most of the time this information is slipped in skilfully enough, and many children find it fascinating:

Promising cheerfully that no feast could spoil his appetite for her cakes, Nicholas followed her indoors. A table, fashioned roughly from a tree trunk, held the remains of Meg's cooking, a big bed was built into the wall, and on pegs by the door hung the shepherd's cloak, the tar-box and searing iron with which he doctored his flock, his lantern and his spare crook. It was all warmly familiar, and Nicholas stooped to pet one of the delicate lambs that lay bedded in hay in a corner.

This description (from *The Woolpack*), thoroughly acceptable in its context, is illustrated by a clear line drawing of the shepherd's tools, a device frequently used to help to convey more clearly a picture of the times. You can trace, too, through the various books, the slow changes in the London streets and in the manners and customs of the different generations. But it must be admitted that this piling up of detail does not always succeed in its purpose: sometimes it gets very much in the way, as in the long account of the apprentice system, given in *Ring Out Bow Bells* to two young people whose own lack of interest may well be echoed by the reader. A similar situation is dealt with more expertly in *The Writing on the Hearth*. Master Simon is here explaining student life to Stephen, as the boy gets his first glimpse of the spires of Oxford. Stephen, who longs to enter Oxford as scholar, is absorbed in the narrative, and the reader's interest naturally goes along with him.

But the question here is not merely a matter of local failure or success in technique: it involves one's reaction to the tone and style of all the stories. For Cynthia Harnett's books are quite distinctive in this respect: she seems to find detail more easy to handle than emotion. So her physical reconstruction of the period, though historically accurate, lacks the warmth and enthusiasm of Rosemary Sutcliff's writing. You do not really feel your way into the lives and thoughts of Cynthia Harnett's England as you enter into the spirit and values of the Britain of *The Eagle of the Ninth* or *Warrior Scarlet*. This in itself, of course, gives her books a greater appeal for the younger age-range, the ten to twelve-year-old, for whom the Sutcliff books are often still too emotionally mature–even frightening. The Harnett books are quieter, less complex, less disturbing: but full of interest and adventure nevertheless. And besides giving an insight into the lives of an earlier century they do involve the reader also in the perennial concerns of the young adolescent. The concerns of Bendy, in *The Load of Unicorn*, for instance, are those of any youngster of his age; how to reconcile his own personal loyalties with what the adult would expect of him, and, more seriously, how to understand and judge for himself the uneasy mixture of motives which governs his own conduct. This growing awareness of himself is shown in several incidents in this book: first in the events following Humphrey's mean attack on the blind old woman:

In a flash Bendy was after him. He caught him before he rounded the corner and dragged him back by the neck of his tunic. He was too angry to know just how he did it, but he pushed Humphrey down and held him there until he had collected the scattered beads out of the muck. Then for good measure *and in payment of his own account* [my italics], he rolled him over into the flowing kennel and left him spluttering. That done, he gave the old woman the tray and tried to rub the beads down. . .

This awareness of his own less creditable motives is underlined, later, when Bendy is rebuked and sent to bed for his behaviour. 'He respected his father's justice, for he had enjoyed punishing Humphrey, though Humphrey had well and truly earned it, the little lick-spittle.' Later still in the book, his temper once more gets the better of him, and he knocks Humphrey down the ladder and is forced once more to face himself.

'Fell!' repeated Matthew, 'fell! You threw him down. It was a fall to break his neck. You hate him: you set on him savagely but two days since. The poor child has gone in terror of you. And now that he is to be your brother, and share with you, you have murder in your heart.' Appalled, Bendy shook his head. All his defences had suddenly crumbled, for he knew it was partly true.

Alongside this growing awareness of himself Bendy becomes increasingly critical of the adult world around him. This is the time of Caxton and of the new printing presses, and Bendy is forced to recognise that his step-brothers resist the new machines not because they threaten that craftsmanship in book production which was his father's pride, but solely because, like the machinery of the Industrial Revolution later on, they threaten the established scrivener's livelihood. *The Woolpack* takes further this element of crisis in the life of its young hero. In this book, Nicholas, the wool merchant's son, grows from carefree childhood in his shepherd foster-home to the demands and responsibilities imposed on him first by an over-ambitious mother, but eventually accepted willingly as he becomes personally involved in learning about his father's business and in defending his father's good name. This part of the story is feelingly written. We see what it means to the young Nicholas to leave the freedom of the shepherd's hut and the hill-sides, and to conform instead to his mother's exacting and over-nice notions of courtesy and cleanliness. We sympathise with him as he is torn between the ease and warmth of the shepherd's hut and the colder formalities of his own home, and as he recognises sadly both that his foster parents' growing lack of ease with 'the young master' and his mother's scornful anger when he comes home from a day out with Hal still smelling of the sheep, are forcing him into his new role as the merchant's son and heir. Once he accepts this role we share, too, his startled apprehensiveness at the sudden decision to contract a betrothal for him, and his relief when he discovers that his bride-to-be is still a harum-scarum young girl, who enters wholeheartedly into his adventures with the mysterious Lombards, and eventually helps him to outwit them. In doing so, Nicholas becomes identified with his father's interests, and with his foster brother Hal as his faithful friend and retainer looks forward to his future as 'a man of honour'.

The same care for historical details and the same interest in the child's place in his society are shown in the other books, *Ring Out Bow Bells*, set in Whittington's London, *Stars of Fortune*, concerned with an abortive plot to free Elizabeth Tudor from her imprisonment at Woodstock, and *The Great House*, a wholly domestic story set in the late seventeenth century. This last volume was the first written, published in 1949, and it presents a particular problem of style. There is no direct speech in the book at all; instead, conversation is presented in not-quite-reported speech.

Breathless with running she shook her head. It was no use. Elizabeth had gone out. Just as she came in sight of the house, the black coach drove by, going towards the gates. She could see Elizabeth and her grandmother inside it. So it was no use her going on. They stared at one another helplessly. Suddenly Barbara had an idea. She seized Geoffrey's arm and pointed across the road to the inn. Look! There was Jenny, Mrs Jarvis' daughter. She'd just arrived. Perhaps she had the afternoon off because my lady had gone out. She was such a nice girl. She might be able to help.

This kind of writing is simple and even reasonably lively to read, but could be off-putting for an age-range which usually likes books with 'plenty of conversation'. In the other books normal dialogue is used, speeches being usually fairly straightforward, and given their other-century flavour only by an occasional "tis' or "twas', or by the use of words or phrases like 'the shipmaster', 'scarce an hour's delay', 'plying his boat', or 'you meddlesome little lack-wit'. Only in *The Writing on the Hearth* is the dialogue more determinedly archaic. But this, the latest written of the books (though historically the second in the quartet), is in general the most assured and most ambitious, and is likely to appeal to a more mature audience than the other stories. For although its concerns are in some respects the same—there is the same historical detail, and the same awareness of the problems of the young boy growing up—the main theme is the more abstract problem facing the hero, the need to distinguish good from evil. This problem was foreshadowed in *The Load of Unicorn*, in Bendy's attempts to reconcile himself to the disparity between the stories of chivalry written by his admired Sir Thomas Malory, and his discovery that the Knight's own life and actions were somewhat questionable. His distress at this discovery comes late in the book, when he protests vehemently, 'Sir, he couldn't have been as bad as that if he wrote my book. Look at the way he speaks of chivalry; look at his story of the Holy Grail.' But in this book the question is raised only to be forgotten in the hurry of the story; in Bendy's own excited and triumphant return to his new life with Caxton. In *The Writing on the Hearth* this dilemma is the heart of the story, and is not to be so easily brushed aside. Good and evil are interwoven in the characters of most of the main people of the book. Dame Alice, kind and considerate to Stephen, loyal and loving to her lord, de la Pole, is yet rash and foolish enough to send a letter to her stepdaughter which could cost her husband his life; de la Pole, at first seen as a peremptory and hasty-tempered overlord, nevertheless has a surprisingly thoughtful awareness of the complexities of Stephen's problem; Bolingbroke, the traitor plotting to kill the King by witchcraft, is yet eloquent in his devotion to learning and book wisdom; Meg, the old woman whom Stephen loves and who has proved so unfailingly kind to himself and his sister, is seen to meddle in matters which seem perilously like witchcraft; and Stephen himself, generous and compassionate and passionately anxious to find out and to do the right thing, is betrayed first into deceit and disloyalty to the patroness he loves, and finally and appallingly into agreeing to betray old Meg to death and torture. In the end, of course, he cannot see her hurt; in de la Pole's words 'he is soft of heart', and so fails in his duty. But the questions of good and evil still trouble him. 'To know good from evil is man's hardest task,' said de la Pole. ''Tis the lesson we come into the world to learn.'

'You can set yourself to *learn*,' said the chaplain at the end of the book. 'That is as much as any of us can do.' And with these two confirmatory pieces of advice Stephen has to be content, and the reader must be content too. This requires, of course, a more sophisticated reader, who will not demand the certainty of attitude and judgment displayed in the other books. And perhaps at this stage Cynthia Harnett herself may be achieving a greater maturity and a greater emotional involvement with her books. Certainly her young readers will look forward eagerly to the next volume, for though the audience for these books is perhaps limited, yet they do attract an enthusiastic and faithful readership. They are full of interest, with well-organised plots, with action and adventure of the kind to appeal to the ten to twelve-year-old, and with a thoughtful involvement in the life and problems of the young heroes (and occasionally heroines) of an earlier century.

(1974)

Books by Cynthia Harnett

Historical Books

Fiction

The Great House Methuen, 1949
The Woolpack Methuen, 1951 (Carnegie Medal)
Ring Out Bow Bells Methuen, 1953
The Green Popinjay Blackwell, 1955
Stars of Fortune Methuen, 1956
The Load of Unicorn Methuen, 1959
The Writing on the Hearth Methuen, 1971

Non-Fiction

A Fifteenth-Century Wool Merchant ('People of the Past') OUP, 1962
Monasteries and Monks Batsford, 1963

In collaboration with G V Stokes

In Praise of Dogs Country Life, 1936
David's New World. The Making of a Sportsman Country Life, 1937
Junk the Puppy Blackie, 1937
The Pennymakers Eyre and Spottiswoode, 1937
Velvet Masks Medici Society, 1937
Banjo the Puppy Blackie, 1938
To Be a Farmer's Boy Blackie, 1940
Mudlarks Collins, 1940
Mountaineers Collins, 1941
Ducks and Drakes Collins, 1942
Bob-tail Pup Collins, 1944
Sand Hoppers Collins, 1946
Getting to Know Dogs Collins, 1947
Two and a Bit Collins, 1948
Follow My Leader Collins, 1949
'Pets Limited' Collins, 1950

Russell Hoban:
Returning to the Sunlight

by

IAN D MACKILLOP

Sodden and heavy with the silt of the bottom, they broke the surface, burst splashing into the sunlight, and went skittering across the turtle rocks. 'Summer people!' hissed the turtles, and plopped into the water in rapid-fire order...The mouse and his child lay in a puddle on the stone as the water drained out of them...The sunlight seemed intolerably bright, and its warmth on their tin was delightful. *The Mouse and his Child*, Chapter Six.

RUSSELL HOBAN's current phase of work began about five years ago. The books that belong to this phase are *Kleinzeit*, *The Lion of Boaz-Jachin and Jachin-Boaz*, and *Turtle Diary*. These are full-length novels to which should be added the brief fable which precedes them, *The Sea-Thing Child*. Although short it is not specifically for children. All Hoban's books of the sixties were. They consist of short texts and pictures, suitable mainly for children of less than about eleven. The single exception was his full-length novel, *The Mouse and his Child*, finished in 1966, which may be read by, though was not exactly written for, adolescents. Despite the new departures this is probably still Hoban's best-known book.

The books of the seventies are related to the earlier ones: *The Mouse and his Child* was a kind of creative spending-spree after which Hoban began to think more deeply about his purchases. But anyone who knows the whole run will agree that there has been liberation rather than straight development, a change of method and use of a new kind of art. The current novels are not 'children's books', though all could be read by teenagers. *Turtle Diary* and *The Lion of Boaz-Jachin and Jachin-Boaz* are the most straightforward; *Kleinzeit* is slightly harder with its less distinct narrative line (part of the point, in fact), but it is very funny. To prevent new readers being bothered by this title I should add that it refers to the hero of the book, Morris Kleinzeit (i.e. Small-time). Any reader of *The Mouse and his Child*, and of the early small-children's Hobans, would be drawn in. It would make a good book for discussion, especially of the intervention of the characters 'God' and 'Words', provocative of thought about God, words, and novels as well.

I have been explicit about the timing of this essay because it is as well to stress how recently Hoban has made new departures. He is going to matter for work which in 1976 is quite new and challenging. One thing challenged, for example, is judgment of the earlier books. I must say that *Kleinzeit* made me think *The Mouse and his Child* less good in one way but more serious in another. In the first place some parts seemed to me slightly pretentious, embarrassing even, in a manner that might be illustrated by reference to some remarks from Hoban himself appended to the Puffin edition. Hoban is describing the little clockwork mouse-and-child which inspired his book:

Such pathos in that little action! Many clockwork toys have that quality, but none so much as this particular one. And these toys, whether covered with fabric or plush, or with the tin exposed, are always made in two halves that never fit together exactly. I find that touching, and not irrelevant to the human situation.

When I only knew *The Mouse and his Child* this sounded too much like one of the reptile or mammalian philosophers and (I fear I found) phonies who are encountered by the refugee clockwork toy on its travels. There is the Muskrat: 'I'm always looking for the Hows and the Whys and the Whats. That's why I speak as I do. You've heard of Muskrat's Much-in-Little, of course?' And there is the Turtle, C Serpentina, thinker, scholar, playwright, voice of swamp and pond. I liked the doings and dicta of this crew well enough, but felt occasionally like Neaera H, protagonist of *Turtle Diary*, who says that 'The Windhover' seems in some moods to be a wet poem and twittish. Having read the later books it seems to me that what I thought amusing but arch could more accurately be described as a shy way of broaching things that come out more truly later. It should be added that though the author may be shy about the status of the ideas he is broaching, this does not mean that the style of *The Mouse and his Child* is tentative. Actually it is garrulous and–this is the thing that appears less good with hindsight–even laboured.

The books in Hoban's new phase are also challenging in another way. In each of the four mentioned except *Kleinzeit* the consciousness of the protagonists is confronted and so is that of the reader. They are meant to shake our angle of seeing and it takes time to see if the effects are permanent. The effects must necessarily take root slowly because they express experience that is far from easily obtained. If, for instance, we could take in the burden of *The Lion of Boaz-Jachin and Jachin-Boaz* quickly it would hardly have been worth writing. So I am unwilling to think of some of my doubts about that book as final, doubts which at present centre on the figure of the Lion itself which remains for me an enigma. But since that figure erupts mysteriously into the consciousness of the novel's protagonists its full meaning cannot be expected to be quickly explicable to the reader. The difficulties presented do not always bring up doubts as to quality. One of the most moving and absorbing moments of *The Lion of Boaz-Jachin and Jachin-Boaz* concerns the young man, Boaz-Jachin. This exchange takes place between him and a transient girl friend:

'Daughters are supposed to attract their fathers, sexually...but I don't. I'm not beautiful to him either. He once told me that boys would love me for my mind. In some ways he's rotten.'
'My God!' said Boaz-Jachin. 'I am so sick and tired of fathers.'

Perceptions about the father-child nexus are basic to this book, but their whole point and relation to the Lion theme are still unclear to me.

Another instance of difficulty might be cited from the Boaz-Jachin thread in *The Lion of Boaz-Jachin and Jachin-Boaz*. The young man is seduced by a middle-aged woman who at the point of going to bed attacks him with her fists. The violence seems right, but what does it mean? Possibly it is related to the fight in *Turtle Diary* between William G and a fellow lodger, which in turn may be related to the 'doing a natal' episode in which Ruby, the 'Original Therapist', physically induces a number of people into re-enacting their birth spasms, and that episode in its turn is part of a thought about getting free meaning getting back to primal water. It is not too hard to set down a formula in which some quantities correspond to episodes in this book and others, but the books deserve better than blackboard work.

Having said so much of difficulty it is about time to show what is immediately delightful about Hoban's fiction, to give a hint of its feel.

Hoban has hatched one character whose fame has exceeded his own. His classic figure for children was Manny Rat who made a sleazy début in *The Mouse and his Child*. His return in a sequel has been promised in some remarks which throw light on one facet of Hoban's gifts. In the sequel, he says:

Manny Rat reassesses his life after a student revolt at the Last Visible Dog where he is teaching 'Tinkering 1' and 'Salvage and Repair (Advanced)'.

More of the Last Visible Dog in a moment; at present I only want to suggest that Tinkering, Salvage, and Repair is something Hoban himself is at home with. Yvor Winters once said that there is a certain sort of New Englander 'in which ingenuity has become a form of eccentricity; when you encounter a gentleman of this breed you cannot avoid the feeling that he may at any moment sit down on the rug and begin inventing a watch or a conundrum'.

There is something of this in Hoban: I doubt that he would have trouble with a watch or a timepiece fashioned out of bits from a muddled and oily drawer; and his handiness with a conundrum is proven. He likes to describe mechanical workings in his prose and in his verse. Here are a few lines from the title poem of *The Pedalling Man*, a collection of verses:

A weather vane was what he was–
Cast iron man with a sheet iron propellor, riding a
Worm gear, holding a little steering wheel,
Iron legs pumping up and down–show him a
Wind and he'd go.

The worm gear is just what Hoban would notice. In the novels mechanism is intermeshed with metaphysics; Hoban strains to make sense of his instinct for both. The instincts are brought together in the following remarks:

Laminar flow is the way the water moves past a swimming dolphin. If you make a wooden model of a dolphin, as yacht designers make models when designing hulls, and if you towed that model in a tank to test the speed potential of the design, you would find that the wooden dolphin, with equivalent propulsion, could not attain the speed of the live dolphin. That is because subcutaneous sensors and reflexes keep the live dolphin rippling constantly with the water flowing past it. There is almost zero turbulence, the flow of the water is laminar, and there is optimum swimming efficiency. Sometimes we can feel like that...

(The idea of a wooden dolphin is a characteristic touch.) Here the mechanic form is set against the natural one, the fully functioning form. This form and its movement cannot properly be called metaphysical. It is certainly not so for the dolphin, or, for that matter, for a plant of the order *Laminariacae*, which according to my dictionary has no definite leaves 'but a plain ribless expansion, which is neither simple or cloven'. But Hoban is writing analogic- ally of human beings and meaning to bring out an ideal ease or adaptability which is ill-obtained by them, or not at all, with their habitually used equip- ment. In Hoban's books we frequently find people who are not quite going –the mouse-and-child, who need to be self-winding, Kleinzeit–'It's probably nothing, eh?...Just this little twinge from A to B.' 'Best see where we are with this,' said Dr Pink. 'Run off a few tests, that sort of thing. Nothing to worry about.' In *The Lion of Boaz-Jachin and Jachin-Boaz* the middle-aged Jachin-Boaz finds that he has stopped waking up with an erection. All of them win in the end, though self-winding, coming through the tests, and having an erection in the morning is far from the whole of the matter. Kleinzeit, for example, attains something like 'laminar flow'. The descrip- tion of it says a little about the total field of Hoban's thought:

Kleinzeit took a bottle of black ink and a fat Japanese brush out of the plain deal table drawer. He took a piece of yellow paper, dipped the brush in the ink, poised it over the paper.

You can do it, said Death.

Kleinzeit touched the paper with the brush, drew in one smooth sweep a fat black circle, sweet and round.

That's it, said Death. My present.

Thank you, said Kleinzeit. He tacked the yellow paper to the wall near the clock. Let's go for a walk, he said.

The closing cheerful note is common and attractive in the recent Hoban books, despite the undertow of anxieties. Kleinzeit succeeds in fashioning a right line, becomes a true artist for a moment. Not all the Hoban protagonists are artists, writers, or performers, but many of them are: Neaera H, a children's writer in *Turtle Diary*, Jachin-Boaz, not an artist but a map-maker in *The Lion*, the fiddler-crab in *The Sea-Thing Child*. I should not make too much of this theme, except to say that it is extremely amusingly done: for example, in *Turtle Diary*, 'The best bird drawings I've done were for *Delia Swallow's Housewarming*, one of my early books. The story was rubbish but the swallow was well observed, she was a distinct Laura Ashley type.' A thought does come up, though, about Hoban's type of artistry. I have said that he has an instinct for the mechanic and for the metaphysical. One of his skills, story-telling, may be brought under the first head and it might be said that there is a conflict or a play between this skill and other means of expression. Hoban is an almost *vulgarly* good story-teller, something not always to be found in writers who have begun by working for children and then broadened out. The books do not all have sharply progressive narrative lines, but they are especially rich in yarns within the overall tale–see the pupa to dragonfly episode in *The Mouse and his Child* or, in the new style (much more pithy), Chapters 14 and 18 of *The Lion*. Two examples of special interest may be mentioned, both of effectiveness, but one which is successful in terms of meaning and one which is not. When Jachin-Boaz makes his sortie to the Lion that materialises in the dawn streets of an unnamed metropolis, he takes 'a paper-wrapped package, put in a carrier bag'. The package is of meat which the Lion devours, and is seen to by Jachin-Boaz but not by the onlookers ('Then the meat jerked and jumped about...and tore itself up and disappeared. Then you screamed and jumped in the river.') It seems to me that to withhold the information that the package contains meat is a gratuitous piece of story spinning. Why should we have to wait to find out? By contrast, the successful piece of story-telling is in *Turtle Diary*, Chapter 11. William G visits the zoo and approaches the keeper of the aquarium:

'Suppose,' I said, 'some sort of turtle freak decided to steal the turtles and put them

back in the ocean. What would he need for the job?'
'You're talking about me,' he said.

Our expectations of a hitch are beautifully foiled. This sort of beauty becomes an attribute of the whole book because our overall expectation of a climax begins to be foiled or diverted: another story seems to enter at the end. William G registers a pang of fright:

I'd always assumed that I was the central character in my own story but now it occurred to me that I might in fact be only a minor character in someone else's. Miss Neap's perhaps. And I didn't even know the story.

(Compare *The Sea-Thing Child*: in it the Albatross says to the Sea-Thing Child, who is fearful of the ocean: 'What *isn't* small compared to the ocean! The blue whale's the biggest thing that swims, and that's small in the *ocean*.') At the end *Turtle Diary* begins to take a new shape as the action completes itself.

It is time to bring up one of the subjects promised earlier, the Last Visible Dog problem which occurs in *The Mouse and his Child*. That book has two dogs, two Bonzos. One of them is real and belongs to a tramp who appears at the beginning; he mends the abandoned mouse-and-child toy and sets it on its odyssey. The tramp reappears at the end to see the toy and its friends with fortunes made. At the beginning he enjoins the toy, 'Be tramps', and at the end, 'Be happy'. He frames the story: indeed it might almost be called 'The Tramp's Dream', though there is no explicit indication that this is how it should be taken. It could also be argued that the later books explore the tramp's side of things or the experience of life that lies behind his cryptic injunctions. The other dog is on the label of a tin of dog-food which shows a dog holding a tin of dog-food on the label of which is a dog...and so on. The problem of what lies beyond the last *visible* dog runs through the story and the image has two messages relevant to the later books. They are contra-dictory messages. (Appropriate, if Hoban is really alluding jokingly to the psychologists' Ponzo illusion: two horizontal lines of the same length are set between slanting lines, e.g. railway lines, that could continue to infinity: the upper horizontal line always looks longer than the lower one.)

The first message may be deduced when the child-mouse cracks the prob-lem. Trapped down in river ooze he has plenty of time to study the label on a sunken tin, and with the help of Miss Mudd, a dragonfly pupa, he even-tually sees that beyond the last visible dog there are merely print dots and beyond them blank white space, emptiness that seemed to flow back towards him. What, they wonder, is on the other side of *that*? They decide they are big enough to find out, so with her jointed lip Miss Mudd tears off the label, revealing shiny tin and the mouse-child's reflection of himself. 'There's nothing beyond the last visible dog but us...Nobody can get us out of here. That gives us Why. Now we have to figure out the Hows and Whats.'

Mettlesomeness of this kind is common in the books. Hoban likes heroes, of some sorts.

Heroes who can do something well are still considered necessary for children. And if many of today's books for grownups offer us a selection of the infirm and the awkward, the losers who lap up defeat like chicken soup ladled out by a Jewish-mother kind of fate, we need those too...I think that heroes who excel and win all kinds of good things are the best kind. Myself–I can't use a mythology in which there is nothing to win and consequently nothing to lose.

Hoban's heroes are triers who do excel, if unwillingly. Kleinzeit takes on the hospital into which he has to go and has a love-affair with the ward Sister ('Only a hero would say that Kleinzeit means hero,' she says). Jachin-Boaz leaves his family in quest of a Lion, the idea of which has been planted in his mind by a chance remark of his son's, who also takes up the quest: ultimately the Lion is faced up to by both of them. The protagonists of *Turtle Diary*, William G and Neaera H, conspire to steal green turtles from the London Zoo, to release them from the west country so they can swim to breed on Ascension Island. The books are not about solo figures; the excelling is done often in collaboration, is a dual matter like Miss Mudd's and the mouse-child's solution of the dog-problem (this pair should be compared with William G and Neaera H): in *Kleinzeit* we have the tramp as *alter ego* of Morris Kleinzeit and in *The Lion* the urge outwards is shared by father and son. I was not surprised to read that one of Hoban's favourite stories is Conrad's *The Secret Sharer*.

The protagonists do not like being heroes but their persistence does win for them 'all kinds of good things' the description of which gives one of the books' distinctive flavours. Hoban is especially good at rendering *pleasure*: note, for example, the chapter called 'Now Playing' in *Kleinzeit*. This goes with the book's bounce: you could say they sound like the mouse-child saying, 'Now we have to figure out the Hows and Whats'.

The other message of the Last Visible Dog problem that is relevant to the later books relates to the problem itself rather than to the mouse-child's plucky response to his discovery. It is slightly at odds with the response, because the response is energetic, determined, heroic, and so individualistic, whereas the message that derives from the problem is anti-individualistic. That problem is one of defining 'the present'. What, or where, is the real dog? And when is now? The books are very much concerned with what cannot be subsumed into an idea of the present, of time-scales that impinge on the individual, of urges beyond those of which he is presently conscious.

In all of us, I think, there remains some awareness, rudimentary and inchoate, far down, dim in green light through the ancient needs and tasting of primal salt, in which there is no 'I', no person, no identity, but only the passage, moment by moment, of time through being undisturbed by birth or death. We push away from it but it is there, containing self and struggle both. I think we have to learn to feel for it, to go beyond our swimmer's fright, to dive for it and touch it before returning to the sunlight and the present, to touch it as a child in a dark room gets out of bed to touch the clothes tree that bulks monstrous in the dimness, magnetic with terror.

Hoban is describing a longing on the part of the animate human being for the inanimate, the peace of the pre-animate–as he says, Freud's death-wish. 'We have to learn' to go back through the sea, the ooze, defeat our frights and have the nerve to touch the inert horror, the thing that still has a grasp on us, defeat, perhaps, our desire to be things. The account relates not only to what Hoban's fiction is about but also to what it is like: it shows the potential metaphors in some of the earlier stories. The monstrous clothes tree is to be found in *Bedtime for Frances*. The account describes in general how forces grasp the present. One force that specifically does so for the writer is language: the writer has to reconcile his sense of the realness of the present with the drag back of words, and this is delightfully dramatised in *Kleinzeit*, a fable on this subject. 'Fable' may not do justice to the frenetic, the witty in the book:

Yes, said Word. My mind is full of every kind of nonsense. Something like the way odd tunes and scraps of things get into human minds and sing themselves over and over again, but vastly faster.
Barrow full of rocks? said the yellow paper.
That's just my name for it, said Word. A pneumatic.
Mnemonic, said the yellow paper.
Whatever you like, said Word. The line itself is by Pilkins.
Milton? said the yellow paper.

Bossy and engagingly disorganised Word shows what peremptory demands past makes on the literary artist. But Word is still dependent on the artist and needs his present work to make sense of him.

In this essay it is perhaps apt that while wishing to promote the excitement of the new books I have found it difficult to get away from the Hoban of the sixties. They are beginning to make more sense as the new books come out: even so modest an early work as *Tom and the Two Handles*, a *genre*-piece for children, looks slightly different after parts of *Turtle Diary*. Indeed, Hoban's one book of the fifties looks different now. *The Atomic Submarine* of 1959 was about the new long-range submersion powers of submarines when diesel power was replaced by nuclear generators. One of the mythical figures that Hoban currently finds he can use is that of Orpheus. He was, says the sullen Hospital in *Kleinzeit*, 'a strong swimmer'.

(1976)

Books by Russell Hoban

Herman the Loser World's Work, 1972. First published USA, 1961

The Sorely Trying Day World's Work, 1965. (USA, 1964)

Tom and the Two Handles World's Work, 1966. (USA, 1965)

What Happened when Jack and Daisy Tried to Fool the Tooth Fairies (Initial Teaching Publishing, 1965; Four Winds, 1966). Text in i.t.a.

The Story of Hester Mouse who Became a Writer. And Saved Most of her Sisters and Brothers and Some of her Aunts and Uncles from the Owl World's Work, 1969. (USA, 1965)

Henry and the Monstrous Din World's Work, 1967. (USA, 1966)

Charlie the Tramp Four Winds, 1966

The Little Brute Family Macmillan, 1966; Pan (Piccolo), 1973

Goodnight World's Work, 1969 (USA, 1966)

The Stone Doll of Sister Brute Macmillan, 1968; Pan (Piccolo), 1973

Ugly Bird Macmillan, 1969

Harvey's Hideout Parents' Magazine Press, 1969; Cape, 1973

The Mole Family's Christmas Parents' Magazine Press, 1969; Cape, 1973

Emmet Otter's Jug-band Christmas Parents' Magazine Press, 1971; World's Work, 1973

The Sea-Thing Child Gollancz/Harper, 1972

Letitia Rabbit's String Song Coward McCann and Geoghegan, 1973

Ten What? A Mystery Counting Book Cape, 1974

How Tom Beat Captain Narjork and his Hired Sportsmen Cape/Atheneum, 1974

'La Corona and the Tin Frog', 'The Tin Horseman', 'The Night Watchman and the Crocodile', 'The Clock', in *Puffin Annual Number 1* Penguin, 1974

Dinner at Alberta's Crowell, 1975

A Near Thing for Captain Narjork Cape/Atheneum, 1975

Crocodile and Pierrot. A See the Story Book Cape, 1975

'The Svalomino Affair', in *Cricket* (July 1976)

Books about Frances the Badger

Bedtime for Frances Faber, 1963 (USA, 1960)

A Baby Sister for Frances Faber, 1965

Bread and Jam for Frances Faber, 1966

A Birthday for Frances Faber, 1970

Best Friends for Frances Faber, 1971

A Bargain for Frances World's Work, 1971. An 'I Can Read' book

Egg Thoughts and other Frances Songs Faber, 1973

Novels

The Mouse and his Child Faber, 1969

The Lion of Boaz-Jachin and Jachin-Boaz Cape/Stein and Day, 1973

Kleinzeit Cape/Viking, 1974

Turtle Diary Cape, 1975

British Picture Books since 1960

by

DENNIS SAUNDERS

IN THE past fifteen years or so there has been an extraordinary increase in the number and quality of picture books for children published each year. Just as the children's novel has attracted the rich and diverse talents of writers who might otherwise have addressed themselves only to the adult reader, so many gifted artists have found personal pleasure and professional satisfaction in devoting at least some of their creative energies to the design of the picture book. As Roger Duvoisin, an experienced illustrator of children's books, said some years ago in a lecture on children's book illustration:

The modern picture book...is also a most interesting medium for artists to experiment in with colours and design–to invent to their hearts' content. This is why many talented artists have been attracted to the picture book, not only for the fun of it but also for the opportunities it offers for their art. The result is that the best children's books have become art creations without losing the particular qualities which give pleasure to children.

We can only guess at the impressions made on a child by his early experiences of art in picture-book form, but I would argue strongly that he needs above all to meet as much variety as possible in order to extend his aesthetic experiences and feed his imagination. Such books can be not only a source of great enjoyment, excitement, fun, and satisfaction but also a powerful agent in developing a child's critical faculties. In this essay I have selected a few of the many artists working in this field today, and through that work I have tried to demonstrate the amazing range and variety of the contemporary picture book.

One of the outstanding and to some extent controversial picture artists working in Britain is Charles Keeping. Visually exciting, dramatic, and charged with considerable power, his books provide us with an individual insight into the world of the city. In particular, Keeping chooses his subjects again and again from the houses and streets, the backyards and alleys, the markets and dockyards of East London. One of his most recent books–not a picture book in our sense–is *Cockney Ding Dong*, a collection of the words and music of popular songs from a variety of sources. Many of them originated in the Edwardian music halls, some of them are Cockney street songs. Keeping has provided superlative illustrations for this book. Here are the colourful and eccentric characters of London life, drawn with wit, feeling, and great affection. Their portraits are unsentimental, uncompromising, and so full of vitality the page can scarcely contain them.

Like many artists Keeping has also illustrated other writers' books for children. Rosemary Sutcliff and Henry Treece are among the authors with whom he has worked, but in my opinion some of the most original and disturbing illustrations he has created were those he contributed to *The God Beneath the Sea* by Leon Garfield and Edward Blishen. This is a vigorous and imaginative retelling of the great Greek myths, and Keeping's astonishing black-and-white pictures splendidly complement the text and visually capture the violence and cruelty of the conflicts of the gods. By turns horrific and heroic, tormented and romantic, these illustrations, together with those in the sequel, *The Golden Shadow*, are not only unforgettable, they are perhaps the most strikingly original to appear for many years, and are an example of how art work of the highest quality can not only illustrate the text but intensify its emotional impact.

In 1968 *The Christmas Story* was published. This consisted of the text specially prepared from the gospels of St Matthew and St Luke for the BBC programme Play School, accompanied by the pictures Charles Keeping had originally drawn for television. In their own way these marked an interesting break with the rather conventional illustrations that traditionally appear in young readers' versions of the story of the nativity. Keeping expresses a personal vision of the birth and its mystery.

However, it is for his own picture books where he is both author and artist that Charles Keeping is best known, and it was *Shaun and the Cart-Horse*, the story of a little Cockney boy with a love of horses, that perhaps first drew attention to his talents in this field.

Although this book met critical acclaim–it received a Carnegie Medal Commendation from the Library Association in 1966–it was *Charley, Charlotte, and the Golden Canary* that was to become something of a classic among modern children's picture books. Brilliantly designed illustrations, startling in their use of vivid colour, tell the tale of Charley and Charlotte who live in the same London street. The old houses are to be pulled down and Charlotte's is the first to go. She and her family find a new home high up in a modern block of flats, but Charley's home is spared for the time being and he remains below, lonely in Paradise Street. He never sees his friend, so he buys a canary to take her place and it is the bird that finally brings the two children together again. One day Charley takes it out of its cage and, as a cat springs for it, the terrified canary flies up towards one of the new tower blocks. Straining his eyes upwards Charley suddenly sees his old friend, Charlotte, waving to him from her high balcony—and on her finger is Charley's canary!

There is already an exhilarating freshness and vigour about the illustrations in these early books. Each new page takes the reader by surprise. It is not only the boldness of colour that stimulates the imagination but the daring and freedom with which it is used. One recalls especially the picture of Charley's house standing forlornly alone in what remains of Paradise Street, a mongrel prowling the foreground of the picture; Charlotte playing alone on her high-rise balcony; Charley at home with his canary; the cat pouncing; and the double page that shows Charley straining his eyes against the sun to see his canary and, facing, the child's view of the block of flats towering dizzily above him.

Alfie and the Ferryboat appeared in 1968 and again Charles Keeping projected the world of the East London streets as seen through the eyes of a small boy. Keeping's is a disturbing, individual vision. In these picture books there is colour, joy, and celebration, but the atmosphere is also touched with mystery and fear and a hint of the sinister—qualities that reappear more powerfully in such later books as *Through the Window* and *The Spider's Web*.

Railway Passage portrays the daily life of this ordinary London street. Keeping is on familiar territory here, and the characters who people these pages have a family likeness to those we meet in some of his other books, especially *Cockney Ding Dong*. Each week the tenants get together to fill in their football coupon, and finally their efforts are successful. Together they win and share a fortune, and Keeping's account of what happens to each of them as a result is full of rich humour and sharp observation. Here is an entertaining and totally realistic gallery of East London characters reacting in different ways to their windfall. This book was runner-up for the 1974 Kate Greenaway Medal and it was *Charley, Charlotte, and the Golden Canary* that had been awarded the medal for 1967. In my view, however, *Joseph's Yard*, published in 1969, is perhaps one of the most impressive children's picture books of the last ten years or so. Its story is simple but carries its own moral and, like his other books, encourages the young reader to think beyond the brief text. It is about sharing and the need for freedom.

Joseph is a small boy whose backyard is a place of brick, wood, stone, and rusty old iron. Rain falls, the sun shines, winds blow through it, and the snow covers it, but no living thing grows there. One day a man collects the rusty old iron and gives Joseph a plant in exchange. Joseph pulls up a piece of stone, digs the earth that lies beneath, and carefully places his plant in the ground. The plant thrives but Joseph breaks off the only flower and it dies. 'Joseph was alone again in the yard.' The seasons pass and in the spring the plant comes to life again. It blooms, and this time Joseph leaves the flower to grow. It attracts insects, and birds come because of the insects. Not far behind the birds come the cats. Joseph furiously drives them all away and covers the plant with his coat so that no one else can enjoy his flower. Deprived of sun and rain the plant dies, and Joseph realises that his love and his jealousy have together killed the only beautiful thing he has ever had in his yard. Spring comes again and Joseph, having learnt his lesson, lets the plant grow. 'In time the plant filled the yard. Insects flew among its flowers, birds perched in its branches, cats lay in its shade. And Joseph was happy.'

Joseph's Yard is visually an exciting book. Keeping's style is expressionistic and the pictures are colourful, mysterious, and dramatic. It is also unpredictable. One double page may bear several small pictures of Joseph carrying his plant into the yard, pulling up the stone, digging the earth, while another portrays an enormous sun, or the birds and, most vividly of all, the cats who visit his yard. The violence of Joseph's fury towards these creatures and the stillness of his protectiveness towards the plant are effectively juxtaposed on a double page. Immediately following there is a sudden startling close-up of Joseph's face as he realises what his jealousy has done.

Joseph himself is an ordinary boy–Keeping, indeed, makes him a very plain lad–but his story is a small masterpiece. A Charles Keeping picture book is always an adventurous exploration of colour, design, and form, and usually offers the reader an unconventional and largely unpredictable experience. I believe he is among the most stimulating of today's picture-book artists and the one most likely to open up new territories.

Many picture-book artists develop a fairly consistent style. Their professional development continues and they enjoy the challenge of experimenting with new techniques and media, but on the whole their work has about it an easily recognisable, familiar likeness. In addition to those discussed in this essay one thinks immediately of Edward Ardizzone, John Burningham, Michael Foreman, Raymond Briggs, Gerald Rose, and the exquisite, highly-mannered pictures of Errol Le Cain, all of them creative illustrators whose work deserves to be discussed at length and who could well have featured prominently in any essay on British picture books. In the USA, Maurice Sendak springs to mind, Ezra Jack Keats, Tomi Ungerer, Bill Peet, Roger Duvoisin with his Happy Lion stories and his books about Veronica the hippopotamus and Petunia the goose, Nancy Ekholm Burkert and many others; the Swiss Celestino Piatti and Felix Hoffman, Yutaka Sugita in Japan, and the Austrian Monika Laimgruber, whose visual interpretations of Hans Christian Andersen are among the most beautiful picture books published in recent years. The work of these contemporary artists is as recognisable as that of such figures of the past as Arthur Rackham, Beatrix Potter, and Kate Greenaway herself.

Fiona French, however, is a highly original and talented artist who varies her style to suit the theme and subject-matter of each new book. In this way she not only effectively evokes the period and place in which the story is set but also creates the unique spirit and atmosphere of the tale. Her first book was *Jack of Hearts*, published in 1970. This tells of four kings: the King of Hearts, a happy man who rules the sunny Southland, the rich King of Diamonds who rules the Eastland, the warlike King of Clubs of the Westland, and the evil King of Spades, ruler of the Northland.

Fiona French tells her story through pictures in which the character of the cards is woven into the events of the story, and the medieval flavour of the original designs of our modern playing cards is preserved in the vivid colours and formal design of each illustration.

Huni was inspired by Egyptian mythology and tells how the boy Huni, son of the Pharaoh, undergoes the ordeal that will prove his bravery and demonstrate whether he is suitable to succeed his father as ruler of Egypt. The test consists of a journey along the River Nile through the dark, following the sun god, Ra. Fiona French illustrates this myth in the style of an Egyptian frieze. The characters in the story mimic the formal gestures and positions of the Egyptian originals, and the artist has devoted the same kind of sensitive attention to ornament and pattern, shape and symmetry, as is to be found in the first book.

The Blue Bird is set in seventeenth-century China. Jade Lotus is a young girl who tries to find a cure for her cage bird who has mysteriously stopped singing. Hearing of an Enchantress who can understand the language of birds, she and her friend set out for the Enchantress's palace. On the way they are joined by a tortoise, a cat, and a rain dragon. The Enchantress reveals that she intends to capture all the birds in China and stop them singing by turning them to stone. Hundreds of them already decorate the palace roofs. However, Jade Lotus and her companions overcome the Enchantress's power, and the rain dragon washes away her evil by turning himself into a shower of rain. As the first drops of water touch the stone birds they come to life and begin to sing again, and Jade Lotus decides to free her own singing bird from its cage—a happy touch that shows how even a brief text can unobtrusively make its own moral point. Jade Lotus learns that, like the birds frozen into silence on the palace roof, her own bluebird was simply pining for its freedom.

Until the climax of the story the pages of the book have been rendered almost entirely in blue and white in a formalised style reminiscent of the willow plate pattern, capturing perfectly the still, cold landscape. As soon as the birds regain both their freedom and their singing voices the double page that shows them taking off from the palace roof introduces a scatter of splinters of colour, and the remaining pages show Jade Lotus and her friends returning home through a still stylised but now richly colourful, even exotic, landscape of flowering trees and lakeside reflections.

King Tree takes page design a stage further, and some of the visual effects in this book are quite remarkable. The courtiers of Louis the Fourteenth are acting a play in the Gardens of Versailles. They dress up as trees and each boasts of his fine qualities. Which of them shall be King of the Trees? The court ladies finally choose the orange tree, but before this we have been treated to page after page of boldly coloured and dramatically designed illustrations—one of which, a rather sinister close-up of the courtier playing the vine, has tremendous impact as the unsuspecting reader turns the page— in which the various trees parade their virtues. In more senses than one the book creates an almost theatrical excitement.

Fiona French chose an allegorical tale of good and evil for *City of Gold*. Two brothers decide to fight the Demon that threatens the City of Gold, but each has his own reasons for doing so. In the end the pleasure-loving and deceitful Thomas comes to his senses and, by sacrificing a sack of treasure, saves his brother John from the Demon's fiery cave.

What lends this book a particular interest is the author's concept of the pages as a series of medieval stained-glass windows. The allegorical conventions of the story itself are matched visually by the medieval perspective, the patterned borders, the emblems that show us which is the 'smooth high road' and which the difficult, that assure us that the horse is 'willing to go far', or emphasise the 'greed, sloth, and envy' of the jolly nobleman whom Thomas meets. The overall design and colouring are stunning—the richest of reds predominates in the later scenes which show the struggle with Asmodeus —but, just as one is continually surprised to find some hitherto unnoticed detail in a medieval window that one thought held no more secrets, so there is a good deal to explore in the pages of this book. Almost hidden in the overall design of each 'window' are humorous, touching, and sometimes grotesque details of medieval life.

While *Aio the Rainmaker* draws its inspiration from African culture, Fiona French's most recent book for children, *Matteo*, recalls the splendours of Florence and the lives of the Italian artists and noblemen who lived there centuries ago. The pages glow with warm colours and are filled with details of the costume, decoration, and architecture of the period.

Brian Wildsmith is perhaps one of the best-known names among children's book artists. He has illustrated some of La Fontaine's fables: *The Hare and the Tortoise*, *The Lion and the Rat*, which was runner-up for the 1963 Kate Greenaway Medal, *The North Wind and the Sun*, *The Rich Man and the Shoe Maker*, *The Miller, the Boy, and the Donkey*. Edward Blishen's *Oxford Book of Poetry for Children* is a fine example of how an artist's brilliant use of colour can enrich and extend the poetry anthology.

Bright, cheerful, and contrasting colours–'kaleidoscopic' is the adjective often applied to his work–characterise all Wildsmith's books. The effect is sometimes that of delicate watercolour, sometimes more dramatically impasto. The style has occasionally been cubist, as in *The North Wind and the Sun* and his *Mother Goose* anthology of nursery rhymes, and almost always representational, though he has claimed to have 'abstract tendencies'.

Among his non-narrative books is his unusual alphabet book *Brian Wildsmith's ABC*, awarded the Kate Greenaway Medal in 1962, and the series of three books, *Fishes*, *Wild Animals*, and *Birds*, the last of which was runner-up for the Kate Greenaway Medal in 1967. The same qualities of lively inventiveness, rich colour, and bold shapes characterise his counting book *123*, and *Puzzles*, in which a collection of puzzle pictures pose such questions as 'Can you find the nest that has only one egg in it?' 'How many animals can you see in the picture?' There are also invitations to explore the pictures in other ways, and one feels that this kind of book for very young children is one that could attract the attention of more artists. More recent story books include *Python's Party*, a very amusing and superbly illustrated account of what happens when Python throws a party. Each of the guests shows off in his own way, and then Python demonstrates that he can outdo the pelican in this respect by getting even more animals into his mouth. Things take a nasty turn when he refuses to let them out, but their friend the elephant chances by and frees them by placing his foot on Python's tail.

The Circus consists of a series of beautiful pictures of performing animals, entertainers, and their acts. There is no narrative. *Squirrels* is a simple account of the day-to-day life of these creatures. It has no story but takes the young reader through the seasons and shows something of the squirrel's habits and characteristics. This is a book that contains a good deal of interesting information about the squirrel, but what comes over most memorably is the poetry of the pictures in which Wildsmith depicts this creature with a rare and sensitive delicacy of line and colour.

Pat Hutchins' picture books for children show a strong similarity of style, technique, and design. She often limits herself to certain yellows, reds, pale blues, and greens, though she has on occasion used a much wider range of colours in such books as *The Wind Blew*. Her tidy, but almost fussy, drawings contain those precise details that, carefully chosen, will point up her narrative. Pat Hutchins' creations do have a family likeness. For example, compare the treatment of the animals in such books as *Rosie's Walk*, *Good-Night, Owl!* and *The Silver Christmas Tree*, or the human figures in *Clocks and More Clocks*, *Don't Forget the Bacon!* and *The Wind Blew*. The illustrations in this author's books are characterised by soft, light colours, intricate but clear detail, and a good deal of visual humour. They have an attractive decorative quality, and a warmth and cosiness that appeal to the very young.

Clocks and More Clocks is about the bumbly Mr Higgins, splendidly dressed in swallow-tailed coat, brown checked and striped trousers, and red and black spotted cravat. Mr Higgins has a problem. As he walks from attic to bedroom to kitchen in his home he finds that each of his clocks tells a different time. He enlists the help of a clockmaker who agrees to come round to the house but takes the precaution of bringing with him a pocket watch. Of course, as they move from one room to the next, Mr Higgins compares the time shown on each clock with that on the watch, and finds that all his clocks are right after all. His delightful conclusion is, 'What a wonderful watch!' Needless to say, he buys himself one, and 'since he bought his watch all his clocks have been right'.

There is a good deal of fun in the text of a Pat Hutchins picture book. Judging from *The Surprise Party*, *Good-Night, Owl!* and her recent *Don't Forget the Bacon!* she clearly finds playing with words irresistible. The fun usually arises from confusion over misheard or misremembered messages. Rabbit's announcement in *The Surprise Party* that he is to hold a party for his friends is changed radically and comically as the news is passed on from one creature to another. The story of *Don't Forget the Bacon!* concerns whether or not the small boy will recall exactly what his mother asked him to bring back from the shops. The list is simple: 'Six farm eggs, a cake for tea, a pound of pears, and don't forget the bacon,' but it is hilariously distorted as the boy walks along the street.

It is possible that at least part of the appeal of some of Pat Hutchins' books lies in the fact that the young child reading or sharing them with an older person is sharing, too, a secret that the characters in the story do not know. He is 'in' on something and they are not. He knows about Rosie's danger, she doesn't. He knows why Mr Higgins' clocks appear to be wrong. He knows what Rabbit's original message was, but Rabbit's friends don't. He can also remember what it was that the boy sent shopping was not supposed to forget.

The repetition and accumulation of incident and language which are such important elements in traditional rhymes and folk stories also play a large part in this author's picture-story books, and one can imagine that these are stories likely to be read and re-read with great enjoyment of text and illustration no matter how well known they become. *Rosie's Walk*, Pat Hutchins' first book, is already a classic of its kind.

Refreshing, hilarious, and lively are the adjectives that spring to mind when describing Quentin Blake's work for children. There is a zany, wholly delightful spontaneity that characterises his pictures and, like those of Pat Hutchins, an instantly recognisable family likeness about the people and animals that inhabit the world of his stories. Apparently sketched and coloured at speed, these appealing, cheeky-looking and often wildly underfed figures seem to find their way everywhere, for Blake is a prolific artist and has illustrated many books by other writers. These are usually black-and-white line drawings. His most attractive work is surely to be found in his own picture books and those he has created with John Yeoman and Russell Hoban. He generally works in pen and ink and watercolour, and it seems a medium ideally suited to the world he has created of skinny kids, eccentric-looking adults, raggedy horses and hopeful-looking dogs, and–when villains are needed–gormless-looking and incompetent rogues. His heroes–almost always small boys and girls, though there are one or two exceptions–smile out at us happily, as often as not daydreaming and eternally optimistic. They may not always get things right, but Quentin Blake's boys in particular are intensely practical. It doesn't do to underestimate them.

Patrick and *Jack and Nancy* are two gentle fantasies in which dreams come true, while *Angelo* is a funny-sad story about a boy who could dance on a tightrope and travelled around Italy with his family of entertainers.

Snuff, however, is perhaps the best of the early books. Snuff himself is page to Sir Thomas Magpie, a somewhat down-at-heel knight. They have only one horse between them–a *very* bony Blake horse–and Snuff is not very adept at following lessons on How to Hold a Sword, How to Dance, and How to Bow. On the other hand, he shows how bright he really is by out-witting the thieves who have just robbed the Bootmaker of much of his stock.

Mouse Trouble and the Lester stories are full of lively good humour, detail, and surprise, but one book in particular shows Quentin Blake at his inventive best. Russell Hoban provided the text for *How Tom Beat Captain Najork and his Hired Sportsmen* and seems to have inspired Blake to produce some of his funniest and most memorable pictures. Tom is a small boy who spends much of his time fooling around–with sticks, stones, bent nails, holes in fences, mud, barrels in alleys, and almost anything that comes to hand and for which he can find a use. He lives with his maiden aunt, Miss Fidget Wonkham-Strong, an awesome female who wears an iron hat and takes no nonsense from anyone. 'Where she walked the flowers drooped, and when she sang the trees all shivered.' Happily taking life as it comes Tom eats his mutton and cabbage-and-potato sog, and dutifully learns off pages of the Nautical Almanac which his aunt sets him as punishment. However, she finally decides that the only way to stop his fooling around is to send for Captain Najork and his hired sportsmen. He comes up the river in his pedal boat and challenges Tom to three highly acrobatic and messy contests: womble, muck, and sneedball. In colourful, lively pictures Quentin Blake almost convinces us that these games exist–'When it was Tom's turn to rake he did not let Captain Najork and the hired sportsmen score a single rung, and at the end of the snetch he won by six ladders'–and since Tom is used to shaky, high-up, wobbling, and teetering kinds of games he easily beats his opponents. Muck is played at low tide in the river mud, and Tom has fooled around often enough with mud to be in his element. Like the other games sneedball resembles several kinds of fooling around that Tom is particularly good at and the discomfiture of Captain Najork and his men is complete. The story ends with Tom's aunt marrying Captain Najork in spite of his defeat while Tom advertises for a new aunt and finds one to his liking. The future looks bright for him. Her name is Bundlejoy Cosysweet!

Another adventure concerning the same group of characters is chronicled in *A Near Thing for Captain Najork*.

Victor Ambrus is a Hungarian. Born in Budapest, he was an art student at the Hungarian Academy in 1956 and during the uprising he escaped across Europe and settled in England. He has illustrated many books during the past eighteen years and in 1965 he was awarded the Kate Greenaway Medal for his work in general, but especially for one of his best books, *The Three Poor Tailors*.

Many of Victor Ambrus' own story books are illustrated versions of folk tales from his native Hungary. Ambrus brings to his pictures a delightful wit and comic energy in depicting the grotesque antics of the country folk who play such a large part in the stories.

Brave Soldier Janosh is an old braggart who regales the villagers with tall tales of his exploits at the wars–how he routed the great Napoleon and all his troops, single-handed, and so on–and since most of the villagers are simple men they believe the tall stories he tells. It is a student at the tavern who occasionally sneezes, for in Hungary to sneeze at a story is to say you don't believe it.

The Seven Skinny Goats is a masterpiece of its kind. The village innkeeper unwisely allows the boy Jano to mind his flock of seven goats. Jano has a flute and no one who hears it can fail to dance, so the fat goats dance instead of eating and end the day as seven skinny goats. Everyone in turn is captivated by Jano's tunes and, when the Judge decides that the boy must be rolled downhill out of town as a public nuisance, Jano begs to be allowed one last request. He plays his flute and, of course, all the townsfolk succumb to his magic tunes. Sentence is never carried out.

The scenes in which the flute casts its dancing spell over the goats and the villagers are superbly realised in all their frantic activity, and it is perhaps this kind of illustration that Ambrus does best of all. His pictures are funny and full of movement, his people recognisable characters from folk lore: sly rogues, buffoons, tricksters, bucolic clowns, stout bullying inkeepers, stolid farmers and their plump wives.

Ambrus uses the brightest and sharpest of colours in his work and often combines pastel, ink, and watercolour. In general his figures stand out against a white background with only a line or two of text on each page. *A Country*

Wedding is one of the best examples of his art. It follows the exploits and misfortunes of Bandi the Wolf and Zoli the Fox as they hear that a big wedding is to be held in the village. Ravenous as always, they decide to steal a pair of trousers each and pass themselves off as wedding guests. Although they are at first successful, they are discovered gorging themselves and beat a hasty retreat. Quarrelling and fighting with each other outside town, they are dragged back by the wedding guests and made to sing and dance at the feast.

From the opening scene in which Bandi and Zoli eavesdrop on two old women, every picture in this book is a delight, and especially enjoyable are the faces and expressions of the two rogues. Ambrus captures perfectly their every emotion: greed, cunning, drunken high spirits, astonishment and dismay when they are caught. In this as in all of Victor Ambrus' books the scenes of comic violence are the set pieces and are excellently done.

The variety and range to be found among even such a small group of artists as those whose work has been discussed in this essay are further demonstrated and extended by the book list that follows, itself a highly selective choice. In recent years the artist has certainly come into his own in this field. Not only has the child today an amazingly wide variety of picture-story books from which to choose but the book itself has, I am convinced, been raised to new levels of excellence. I do not share Maurice Sendak's concern that the great illustrators of the past may be pushed out by the flood of new creations, and I cannot believe that he is serious when he says that he would like there to be a moratorium, no more books for perhaps a year, just to get the old books back. Of course there is a back list of superb books for children, but it should be a cause for rejoicing that there is such a plentiful supply of books of quality by contemporary artists.

There is a much greater awareness today of the importance of a child's early experiences and there is sadly much truth in Brian Wildsmith's claim that we have too often 'left all that is good and free in our culture to be brought before the child too late, when his taste has already been formed, maltreated, warped, and destroyed by the everlasting rubbish that is still thought by many to be good enough for children. I hope my picture books will help alleviate this, and perhaps guide them to finer and greater paths.'

I believe we have an unprecedented opportunity today to see that children are introduced to books of quality that will stimulate their imagination, pictures that will enlarge their horizons and provide them with new and satisfying aesthetic experiences. Books to grow on.

Select Book List

In addition to the books already discussed, the following select list illustrates some of the range and variety of outstanding picture books from around the world in the last twenty years. The publication date in each case is the date of the book's first appearance in Great Britain.

Edward Ardizzone *Tim All Alone* OUP, 1956

Jose and Ariane Aruego (text by Robert Kraus) *Milton the Early Riser* Hamish Hamilton, 1974

Raymond Briggs *Father Christmas* Hamish Hamilton, 1973

Nancy Ekholm Burkert (text by Brothers Grimm, translated by Randall Jarrell) *Snow-White and the Seven Dwarfs* Kestrel, 1974

John Burningham *Mr Gumpy's Outing* Cape, 1970

Eric Carle *The Very Hungry Caterpillar* Hamish Hamilton, 1970

Eric Carle *The Mixed-Up Chameleon* Hamish Hamilton, 1975

Michael Foreman *War and Peas* Hamish Hamilton, 1974

Michael Foreman (text by Georgess McHargue) *Private Zoo* Collins, 1975

Felix Hoffman (text by Brothers Grimm) *The Seven Ravens* OUP, 1963

Adrie Hospes (text by Marijke Reesink) *The Magic Horse* Bodley Head, 1974

Ezra Jack Keats *Hi, Cat* Bodley Head, 1971

Jack Kent *Twelve Days of Christmas* Hamish Hamilton, 1973

Monika Laimgruber (text by Hans Christian Andersen) *The Emperor's New Clothes* Hamish Hamilton, 1973

Errol Le Cain *The Cabbage Princess* Faber, 1969

Errol Le Cain (text by Brothers Grimm) *Thorn Rose* Faber, 1975

Leo Lionni *Frederick* Abelard-Schuman, 1971

Graham Oakley *The Church Mouse* Macmillan, 1972

Daihachi Ohta *Raintaro* Blackie, 1973

Helen Oxenbury *Pig Tale* Heinemann, 1973

Gerald Rose *Ironhead* Faber, 1973

Maurice Sendak *Where the Wild Things Are* Bodley Head, 1967

Kozo Shimizu (text by Ann Herring) *The Grateful Crane* Blackie, 1973

Yutaka Sugita (text by Robert and Inge Hyman) *Happy with Hubert* Evans Brothers, 1972

Tomi Ungerer *Zeralda's Ogre* Bodley Head, 1970

Bernadette Watts *Rapunzel* Denis Dobson, 1976

William Mayne

by

EDWARD BLISHEN

MY ODDEST encounter with the works of William Mayne was in the children's section of the public library in Kampala, in Uganda. A very small library grant meant that every book had to stay in circulation until it actually fell to pieces, and there, presenting an unusual spectacle of dilapidation, were many of his many books; and as my eye wandered along the titles, recalling nearly a score of pleasures, I wondered what was made of these sly, witty, enchanted, and very English stories in the middle of East Africa. But then I drifted to wondering, a not uncommon critical cogitation, what is made of them in the middle of England. I didn't pursue that inquiry, and shall do so now only with caution, since there is no reliable means of measuring the general effect of a children's writer on his readers; but I must say I suspect that those who argue that William Mayne is an adult's children's writer and not a children's children's writer are expressing nothing better than guesses.

It is not only more generous, but far more sensible and grateful, to say what a good writer he is, and what a welcome effect he is beginning to have on writing for children here. The effect has not taken the form of imitation; he is strictly inimitable, though easy to parody. (I think he is not guiltless of parodying himself.) But what his writing has shown is that stories for children need not drive straight from opening to end; they can shape themselves by a sort of sly oblique process, emerge sideways and even backwards out of dialogue and hints. In fact, all his stories have strong narrative spines; but they are not rigid ones. He has also come so close to the true nature of children's talk and to the way they feel and think that it must be more difficult than it was for a writer of any sensitiveness to reproduce that blunt form of dialogue, always obviously to the purpose, and that falsely consequent rendering of patterns of young thought and feeling, that are conventions of writing for children. In a sense, Mr Mayne has reminded us of the precise nature of children.

To begin with, children fool with words. It is often a very serious foolery. Most dialogue in most children's books assumes that children use words as adults do (though lively adults, too, toy and fiddle with language part of the

time). To children, much of the vocabulary and phrasing their elders have
come to accept calls for questioning. A mother, in one of Mayne's books,
says that a village wants money, and her small son comments: 'I didn't know
villages wanted money. I thought people wanted money.' And, of course,
children spend much of their time in a world of puns; they ransack words
for jokes and secondary meanings, they put phrases under the strain (which
causes them often hilariously to disintegrate) of literal examination. They
have an alertness, too, to the unsaid things lying behind something said;
they have ears inside ears. William Mayne's stories are full of this pure true
comedy of talk among children, of talk between children and adults (the
adults sometimes exasperated or bemused by it, or without the leisure that
enables the child to give it full attention; though the old, as they are often
portrayed in William Mayne's stories, are seen to have re-acquired their
sense of the intricate meanings of language). And, apart from his purely
comic concern with words, William Mayne understands beautifully that
language is itself part of the adventure of being alive and that, by misleading
or puzzling or illuminating, it can inspire or direct events.

It is perhaps this feeling he has for the role played in life by language–
especially in the lives of children, able to be so attentive–that more than anything makes Mayne a highly original and rare children's writer. He can be
arch, and over-playful, and is capable of, as it were, doodling in the style of
William Mayne; at times (I detected this especially in a recent story, *The
Battlefield*) his children and the way they talk reflect the writer's agility with
words, his inability to leave them alone, rather than their credible selves. He
is an extraordinarily prolific writer–two and sometimes three books a year
since he was first published in 1953. I fancy this causes some of the critical
hesitation about him; a writer of such quality ought not to be so productive.
I find this an odd point of view: there is no reason in the world why sensitiveness should not be combined with stamina. But certainly this large
output is responsible for the passages of doodling and of near-self-parody.
It is also to be seen as a kind of generosity: he has spread his attention over
many audiences, from the youngest to the most sophisticated. And because
to each of those audiences, in each of the varied settings of his stories, he
addresses himself in the same manner, in the tone of this dancing and devious
concern with language (as well as because the structure of his writing is *never*
difficult, and he is indeed a master of the short sentence), I cannot believe
that those who say he is writing over the heads of children, or only for those
with a special taste for words, are analysing the situation correctly. In so far
as there is a resistance to his work, it comes sometimes, I believe, from adults
who cannot imagine that work of high quality might have a wide appeal;
and sometimes from a certain shaping of children's appetites, as readers, that
may have occurred by the time they come to Mayne. The point is that most

writing for children *is* blunt and uninventive in its use of language; and that
children may have come to believe that his is the proper tone of any story
whatever.

I have read William Mayne to the most unlikely audiences–apparently
cheerfully blunt boys in Islington, for example–and have found that, if the
stories are properly presented (and in this case I simply mean if they are read
aloud by someone who enjoys them), they cause great delight. This has its
roots in that use of language I've already discussed–that grave fooling with
language that is an activity of children everywhere. It lies, again, in William
Mayne's witty and perceptive treatment of the life of the senses. From the
moment you enter one of his stories, all your senses are deeply and very precisely involved. A boy shuffling his way through fallen leaves feels he is
walking through an immense plate of corn flakes. A hole dug by children
'gives off darkness, like a reverse torch'. When the splendid Dr Sutherland,
in *Words and Music*, swings into 'huge variations on Hymn 477' on the organ,
he seems to be 'shaking the cathedral windows with the music as if he had
his hands on the glass'. A grandfather observes that being among chattering
women is like 'having sparrows tied to your ears'. Moving through an old
mill, boys 'came out of the dark into the dark. The second dark was wet'.
The noise of thunder is 'like the sound of a half-full football being kicked in
an echoing playground, back and forth from a wall'. Quoting phrases in this
manner may give an impression of purple writing: the beauty of William
Mayne's style is that it is never purple–there is rather this constant deft
attentiveness to the sensations of being alive, usually expressed with a wholly
unstrained wit. My Islingtonians chuckled and imitated.

But what is most important is that all this texture, to which I have found
it necessary to pay attention before looking at anything else–this perpetual
lively alertness to language and to sensations–is wholly at the service of Mr
Mayne's stories. It can be enjoyed for its own sake, but it does not exist for
its own sake. The little group of books he wrote about life in a choir school–
beginning with *A Swarm in May*–stand slightly aside from the rest. They
form a loving tribute to a special way of young life. The stories embody
characteristic themes–the impact on the present of complex mysteries with
their roots in the past, the conflict of attitudes to tradition, the relationships
of the young and their elders–but, to my mind, exist as an achievement
separate from the rest. They include some of William Mayne's best inventions: for example, the family of Pargales, who have tended the fabric of the
cathedral for centuries, and whose notion of time, as of the relation of generations among themselves, has become tied to the enormously leisurely pace
at which stone crumbles, gargoyles weather and fall and must be replaced.
In the other stories, two major preoccupations emerge. One is that of the
treasure hunt, of the search for clues to some mystery that carries the charac-

ters back into the past. This is a common theme in writing for children, but William Mayne handles it in a most uncommon manner. Not only is there his usual teasing obliqueness of narration, at once crystal-clear and devious; but there is also a constant ambiguity that enables a story to be interpreted in the light both of the most sober common sense and of the most extravagant imagination. Fantasy and realism are beautifully enmeshed. This is the manner of stories such as *The Thumbstick, The Rolling Season, The Battlefield*: and is at its best, in my opinion, in *A Grass Rope*, which was awarded the Carnegie Medal in 1957, and in which the various possible interpretations of the near-magical events have their convincing advocate among the characters: a child who believes in magic, a clever boy who brings scientific reasoning to the quest, the children's parents who are simply sensible about it all. The conclusion is perfectly poised: the reader may believe any of the explanations, and perhaps that reader is most worthy of the author who manages to believe all of them. This is a very serious achievement of William Mayne's, I think: to preserve such an active and enchanting neutrality as between all the levels of our experience. Beside this achievement, much writing for children–wholly embracing fantasy or opting for thorough realism–falls awfully short. You might have said my Islington boys were made for realism. So they were: but they were made also for doubt about any single type of interpretation of any human experience whatever, and my impression was that the subtle, exhilarating ambiguity of William Mayne's stories fed this need of theirs. Interestingly, even when Mayne is writing less ambitious stories, as close to plumb realism as he ever comes, the shadow of a proper mystery is allowed to fall upon the commonest things–as surely it does in the lives of all children. An example is a recent story for very young readers, called *The Yellow Aeroplane*, in which a common or garden tower in a wood, in fact a vent for the railway that passes through a tunnel below, is (for the unaccountable smell and sounds it emits) taken to be some supernatural, haunted edifice. A common wood near a common housing estate is touched with that Grimm-like uncertainty and sense of splendid peril which, as much as matter-of-fact realism (which they also love), so often shapes children's response to whatever world is around them.

The second large theme often, but not always, stems from this first one. It is the theme of enormous makings and destructions. The boys in *Sand* find what appear to be the remains of a prehistoric creature under the sand; they set out on an elaborate task of secret rescue, trying to retrieve these mysterious bones. The complications of their labour are vast; and so, too, are its consequences. In *Pig in the Middle*, a group of boys set out to transform an old barge into a seagoing vessel; as in *Sand*, they become intricately involved in the task. One of them, when they have achieved part of it, 'suddenly understood the beginnings of the Bible'. It is this business of

making things–of planning for a construction, or of actually constructing–
that again and again William Mayne celebrates; and again, of course, there
could be few things closer to a child's heart. But so often in these stories
the making leads to a vast unmaking, a catastrophe. In *The Battlefield*, the
children's interest in the old tower in the marshes, the steps they take to
investigate and make use of it, lead to near-fatal consequences, a huge
scene of flood and displacement. The children are in fact warned by an old
shepherd that, with so many forces at work–those of nature and of history,
for example–those exerted by inquiring man may be too much. The attempt
to transform the old barge in *Pig in the Middle* leads to immense disaster again
–or at any rate is closely associated with it: the complete collapse of the mill
buildings in which the barge is housed. It seems to me that this theme of
making and breaking, sometimes separate from the magical theme, sometimes part of it, is again a concern that takes William Mayne close to the
young reader, much of whose own life is devoted to bold constructions and
to curiosity about the consequences of interfering with nature.

It is easy to say that William Mayne is an uneven writer. That must be
true of anyone who writes so much. The comment is sometimes made by
critics who appear not to distinguish between the more ambitious stories and
those that are less serious in intention. It is also easy, and I think quite wrong,
to claim that he is a writer for a highly literate minority; as I have said, I
believe this view is an invention of those who see only the freshness, subtlety
and obliquity of the writing, and do not observe that it is always tied to
stories of considerable narrative strength or that children everywhere have a
delight in verbal ingenuity. These are, in fact, extremely *sensible* stories, and
in my experience are recognised as such by a wide range of children. They
are sensible because the heroes are never improbably heroic, and pure villains
have no more place in the stories than they have in life itself. They are
sensible also because Mr Mayne understands the fluctuating relationships
of child with child, the tangle of emotional attitudes which is part of the
reality of children's lives, and of which so many children's writers seem
inadequately aware. One should add that William Mayne is a brilliant
reporter on the nature of family life, on the role of mums and dads. Parents
impose a framework, but that is not all that can be said about them; one of
the best things about this writer's work is that he understands that, at inter-
vals in their busy round, adults are likely to be as much influenced by their
children as their children are by them. The children of the sixties are fortunate
to possess a writer who can make such robust and copious literature out of
a balance of so many gifts, all of them uncommon.

(1968)

Books by William Mayne

Follow the Footprints OUP, 1953
The World Upside Down OUP, 1954
The Long Night Blackwell, 1955
A Swarm in May OUP, 1955
Choristers Cake OUP, 1956
The Member for the Marsh OUP, 1956
The Blue Boat OUP, 1957
A Grass Rope OUP, 1957 (Carnegie Medal)
Thirteen O'Clock Blackwell, 1957
Underground Alley OUP, 1958
The Thumbstick OUP, 1959
Cathedral Wednesday OUP, 1960
The Fishing Party Hamish Hamilton, 1960
The Rolling Season OUP, 1960
The Changeling OUP, 1961
The Glass Ball Hamish Hamilton, 1961
Summer Visitors OUP, 1961
The Last Bus Hamish Hamilton, 1962
The Twelve Dancers Hamish Hamilton, 1962
The Man from the North Pole Hamish Hamilton, 1963
On the Stepping Stones Hamish Hamilton, 1963
Plot Night Hamish Hamilton, 1963
Words and Music Hamish Hamilton, 1963
A Day without Wind Hamish Hamilton, 1964
A Parcel of Trees Hamish Hamilton, 1964
Sand Hamish Hamilton, 1964
Water Boatman Hamish Hamilton, 1964
Whistling Rufus Hamish Hamilton, 1964
The Big Wheel and the Little Wheel Hamish Hamilton, 1965
No More School Hamish Hamilton, 1965
Pig in the Middle Hamish Hamilton, 1965
Earthfasts Hamish Hamilton, 1966
The Old Zion Hamish Hamilton, 1966
Rooftops Hamish Hamilton, 1966
The Battlefield Hamish Hamilton, 1967
The Big Egg Hamish Hamilton, 1967
The House on Fairmount Hamish Hamilton, 1968
Over the Hills and Far Away Hamish Hamilton, 1968
The Toffee Join Hamish Hamilton, 1968
The Yellow Aeroplane Hamish Hamilton, 1968
Ravensgill Hamish Hamilton, 1970

Royal Harry Hamish Hamilton, 1971
A Game of Dark Hamish Hamilton, 1971
The Incline Hamish Hamilton, 1972
Robin's Real Engine Hamish Hamilton, 1972
Skiffy Hamish Hamilton, 1972
The Jersey Shore Hamish Hamilton, 1973
A Year and a Day Hamish Hamilton, 1976

Collaboration

The Gobbling Billy (with Dick Caesar) Brockhampton, 1969 (originally published by Gollancz in 1959 under the name Dynely James)

Anthologies

The Hamish Hamilton Book of Kings (with Eleanor Farjeon) Hamish Hamilton, 1964
The Hamish Hamilton Book of Queens (with Eleanor Farjeon) Hamish Hamilton, 1965
The Hamish Hamilton Book of Heroes Hamish Hamilton, 1967
The Hamish Hamilton Book of Giants Hamish Hamilton, 1968
Ghosts Hamish Hamilton, 1971

Pseudonymous

The Football, The Lost Thimble, The Picnic, The Steam Roller and *The Tea Party* by Charles Molin, Hamish Hamilton, 1966
Ghosts, Spooks and Spectres by Charles Molin, Hamish Hamilton, 1967
The Swallows by Martin Cobalt, Heinemann, 1972

Mary Norton, Fred Inglis, and the World We Have Lost

by

NIGEL HAND

'...a great arc of writers, formidable and intelligent men and women, ranging from (so to speak) William Mayne or Mary Norton on the right to Helen Cresswell and Mrs Peyton on the left, are in full retreat from their times...'

IN HIS two remarkable and indispensable essays on Children's Literature in *Ideology and Imagination*, Fred Inglis sees the contemporary children's writer as a representative of liberal individualism, trapped in a world which he can no longer cope with. Such values as individual liberty are in constant retreat in the world of bureaucracy and the multi-nationals; and imperatives like 'Be honest and sincere' cannot, when we have lost our sense of significant human ends, tell us what we ought to pursue. A consequence of this state of affairs has been what the sociologists elegantly term 'privatisation'. Or, as Inglis writes:

One reaction has been to pull back into their homes and bolt the kitchen door and hold on to what there is in private. Two consequences have followed. One, an intolerable imprisonment within an over-personalised private life; two, the relinquishing of public and political life to giant anti-human forces whom we all have to resist for the sake, literally, of our children.

Who can doubt that this analysis pours light upon the world of the borrowers; that, indeed, it points to the potent centrality of the myth which Mary Norton has created? Inglis goes on:

In a bitty way we find this reaction expressed, judged, and very occasionally transcended in the best novels now written for children. These books reflect the drastic retrenchment which individual liberty has undertaken since January 1933. In a way impossible to Mark Twain, R L Stevenson, Mrs Hodgson Burnett or even Ballantyne or Henty, they have quit history and society...

If that gives us the measure of the change and the problem, where do we see it 'transcended'? Inglis replies: 'I would say that Mrs Peyton's *Flambards in Summer* and Philippa Pearce's *The Children of the House* make the first showings...' As to Philippa Pearce we can all agree; but I am not convinced by the case that has been made for Mrs Peyton. She doesn't seem to me to be sufficiently responsible to her talent to be able to get into focus, for very long, anything that really matters. Just the reverse I take to be true of Mary Norton. But before making the case, I need to chalk up one more item in Inglis' account.

In what sense, in my opening quotation, are some writers said to be of the 'right' and some of the 'left'? The terms (which may be over-simple) point, I think, to the kind of consolation which each writer constructs for the loss of a fully satisfying social world in the here and now. In *The Nightwatchmen*, for instance, Helen Cresswell cultivates an elegant fantasy about a couple of oh-so-charming drop-outs who are relentlessly pursued by the green-eyed forces of anti-life. If this represents a leftward retreat, then hankering after the past (seen as a world of ordered and stable values) takes us off to the right. In his book *The World We Have Lost*, Peter Laslett attempts to give an account of the feel and shape of social life in the pre-industrial world, in comparison with the early twentieth century. At the end of the first chapter he writes:

Time was when the whole of life went forward in the family, in a circle of loved, familiar faces, known and fondled objects, all to human size. That time has gone forever. It makes us very different from our ancestors.

Laslett's analysis points up unmistakably an underlying 'structure of feeling' in *The Borrowers* quartet. Let us remember that Pod is a cobbler, and that borrowers are craftsmen; that their children become in due course their apprentices–in other words that the family is also the economic unit as it is in Laslett's pre-industrial world; keep in mind that the immensely energetic imaginative life of *The Borrowers* centres in a continual, sometimes desperate, attempt to transform random objects into a knowable environment built on a 'human' scale; add, for atmosphere, the refrain of melancholy–'Where are they now?'–that echoes through the volumes...And is not the formula complete?–Surrender of the world at large to 'giant anti-human forces' consoling itself in a touching, nostalgic attempt to recapture the world we have lost.

To compound the case we have the central characters' sense that they are a dying race. The story is full of references to, even meditations upon, lost forms of life.

Arrietty was glad to see the morning room; the door luckily had been left ajar and it was fascinating to stand at last in the thick pile of the carpet gazing upwards at the shelves and pillars and towering gables of the famous overmantel. So that's where they had lived, she thought, those pleasure-loving creatures, remote and gay and self-sufficient. She imagined the Overmantel women–a little 'tweedy' Homily had described them, with wasp waists and piled Edwardian hair–swinging carelessly outwards on the pilasters, lissom and laughing; gazing at themselves in the inset looking-glass which reflected back the tobacco jars, the cut-glass decanters, the book-shelves, and the plush covered table. She imagined the Overmantel men–fair, they were said to be, with long moustaches and nervous, slender hands, smoking and drinking and telling their witty tales. So they had never asked Homily up there! Poor Homily with her bony nose and never tidy hair...They would have looked at her strangely, Arrietty thought, with their long, half-laughing eyes, and smile a little and, humming, turn away. And they had lived only on breakfast food–on toast and egg and tiny snips of mushroom; sausage they'd have had and crispy bacon and little sips of tea and coffee. Where were they now? Arrietty wondered. Where could such creatures go?

Of course the Overmantels do not belong to the pre-industrial world. We note that revealing epithet Edwardian. As a matter of fact our contemporary children's literature seems to have deep roots in that period in two senses. First, as an image of grace and order it glows (ambivalently) through the work of so representative a writer as Philippa Pearce. Second, and related, our contemporary authors are still drawing on the techniques which the Edwardians developed for writing about, and for, the 'liberated' child. In *Bedknob and Broomstick*, for example, Mary Norton herself seems to begin pretty well where E Nesbit left off. She works the trick of ironic juxta-positions between the ordinary and the magical in very much the same way –through clashes of idiom–and almost as hard, as her predecessor. So we have to say that in various ways Mary Norton's work is haunted by images of the past. There is not only the pervasive feeling for the world we have lost, but the conjuring up of specific forms of life which appear to embody lost satisfactions. That there are thus *layers* of nostalgia in these novels presumably testifies to the strength of the impulse which is at work.

And yet how adequate to the Overmantel paragraph are the terms 'nostal-gia' or 'retreat'? Does not such a one-dimensional argument entirely fail to pick up the complex life of the passage? Would we not, on the contrary, be hard put to find anywhere in contemporary writing for children such supple and assured prose? I suggest at any rate the following propositions: Mary Norton's work is about the uses of imagination. One such use is to recapture the past, whether it be in a positive or negative spirit. In *The Borrowers* volumes this activity appears within a complex whole which articulates various other uses of imaginative thought, all of which are enacted and evaluated against each other, giving rise to a positively ordered sense of human priorities. Placed within this organisation, reaching into the past becomes a creative process wherein grow values with which the present and the future can be met. The Overmantel passage gives us a paradigm illustration of the whole process.

Which may be more than enough to say of a piece of fiction for children. However, consider the central and characteristic effect of the quoted paragraph–how on the one hand we are aware of the Overmantels as evoked by Arrietty's imagination, and how on the other they are unequivocally *there* for us too. (In the author's work as a whole this kind of subtlety gives rise to an element of what can only be called teasing. It has notable implications to which I shall return.) How does this paradox arise? First, the formality, as of a meditation, given in the repetition of 'She imagined...she imagined' and so on, plays against the tone, the 'reality', of the speaking voice ('So they had never asked Homily up there!'). Further, the movement of the speaking voice enacts the turns of Arrietty's thought and, again paradoxically, gives body to what is contemplated. Then, the play of reflected images not only 'places' the self-regard of the Overmantels, the quality of life under contemplation, but also realises the play of Arrietty's imagination itself. The glamour is thus ambiguously 'there'–and imagined. But if Arrietty is seen as projecting her desires into the picture it is yet no surprise that she comes to such cool recognitions at the close. For the extraordinary control of tone and movement gives us above all that core of detachment in Arrietty, which is at the same time the condition of her spontaneity and poise, that is, of her 'imagination'. These values, among others, it is the business of the four volumes to define. (It has to be said that in doing so they do not always avoid naïve romanticism.) If we have these values anywhere expressed in a few words it is when, on one alarming occasion, Arrietty is described with characteristic subtlety as 'too curious not to be brave'.

I have discussed elsewhere the whole range of uses of imagination which are presented in the tetralogy. (*Children's Literature in Education*, No. 7.) Mr Pott's self-healing craftsmanship is set against the ego-driven mimicries of the Platters. In Miss Menzies imaginative self-absorption appears as dreamy wistfulness, but in Mr Pott as an almost dour matter-of-factness. If 'natural' imagination in Arrietty is playful spontaneity, in Spiller it is a technique for survival which leaves no room for play. Crisis evokes endlessly inventive responses from Pod, but a self-protective striking of attitudes in Homily. Above all there is that continual dynamic transformation of objects into a 'human' world which makes the Borrowers themselves such an original product of the imagination. I have had occasion already to give the word 'human' inverted commas. Of course it is an engaging if not over-subtle joke that the Borrowers are, if anything, more 'human' than the 'human-beans' in the story. ('Some say they hunt each other...No kind of creature could be as bad as that!') But the point runs much deeper. The word 'human' actually focuses the preoccupations of the whole work. If the exploration of the uses of imagination is one way into the theme, it is complemented by the rendering of a range of 'human' attitudes to the Borrowers themselves. Each of the human-beings in the story is characterised essentially by the extent of his ability to 'realise' the Borrowers, by the quality of his imagination. A measure is set in that dramatic *tour de force* which constitutes Chapter 9 of the first volume, when the Boy (Mrs May's brother) encounters Arrietty with a perplexed wonder which quite unconsciously acknowledges at the same time that she is just as much a centre of life as he is himself. In a crucial sense he is the most 'imaginative' character in the whole story. By contrast, the decline of life in Aunt Sophie is marked by her failure to see Pod as anything but the product of her own befuddled 'imagination', while Mrs Driver's inability to acknowledge what she 'sees' betokens a fear of life which expresses itself, in turn, in viciousness of impulse. An essentially animal nature, the gipsy Mild Eye inevitably realises the Borrowers as creatures to hunt, capture, and if possible make a quick profit out of; whereas Tom Goodenough's 'good' nature exhibits its genial strength, and its limitations, in his placing the Borrowers roughly in the category of animals he lives with as 'friends'. In the crudely exploitative attitudes of the Platters imagination appears as driven by the ego. But if this manifestation is obviously contrasted with the sensitivity and kindness of Miss Menzies and Mr Pott, then those qualities are tinged with self-consolation in Miss Menzies, and even in Mr Pott are not unmixed with a desire to make use of the Borrowers. Only the Boy has enough imagination, at first, to let Arrietty *be*; but then, of course, he falls into the meddling temptation to do what he 'imagines' to be good.

The pre-eminently human use of the imagination, then, is to create a 'human' world, and that fundamentally entails the imaginative realisation of the humanity both of oneself and others. These bald truths are embodied in the tale. But if the fable evokes criteria for the word 'human', are they adequate? More adequate, in my view, than any offered elsewhere in contemporary children's literature. But do they measure up to Inglis' declaration that 'progressive and individual man (as novelist or teacher) needs some criteria of public right and wrong'? Well, I don't think that Mary Norton overcomes in any decisive way the problems of privatisation and dispossession. Perhaps the most one can say is that in exploring the human uses of imagination she points towards and evokes criteria for the creation of a human world which is *neither* public *nor* private: not public because not set over against the individual, not private because not the *possession* of the individual. But the terms of reference of the children's novelist scarcely permit her to give the problem wide enough definition for a fully satisfying adult 'solution' to emerge.

All the same there is a very impressive range of presented experience in the four volumes taken together. Economy is one of Mary Norton's great gifts. Besides the exploratory techniques already mentioned–Arrietty's recurrent meditations on the possibilities of life, the interacting presentations of human character and of modes of imaginative thought–there is the force of the chief dramatic episodes themselves. Each of the episodes is in fact an exploration of the possibilities of a particular way of life.

Pod was a little irked by his riches; he had never visualised, not in his wildest dreams, borrowing such as this. Homily, he felt, should call a halt; surely, now, their home was grand enough; these jewelled snuff-boxes and diamond encrusted miniatures, these filigree vanity-cases and Dresden figurines–all, as he knew, from the drawing-room cabinet–were not really necessary; what was the good of a shepherdess nearly as tall as Arrietty or an outsize candle-snuffer?

What makes Mary Norton a real artist as very, very few children's novelists are, is that the critic's great question, 'What, ultimately, for?' and intelligent criteria in terms of which an answer comes to define itself, are fully embodied in and evoked by the presented life. When the first crisis in the story begins to develop–is Pod to risk teaching Arrietty how to borrow?–Homily is surprisingly in favour of the idea. (Actually she has, as usual, an ulterior motive.)

'The child is right,' she announced firmly. Arrietty's eyes grew big. 'Oh, no–' she began. It shocked her to be right. Parents were right, not children. Children could say anything, Arrietty knew, and enjoy saying it–knowing always they were safe and wrong.
'You see, Pod,' went on Homily, 'it was different for you and me. There was other families, other children...the Sinks in the scullery, you remember. And those people who lived behind the knife-machine–I forget their names now. And the Broom-Cupboard boys. And there was that underground passage from the stables–you know, that the Rain-Pipes used. We had more, as you might say, freedom.'
'Ah, yes,' said Pod, 'in a way. But where does freedom take you?' He looked up uncertainly. 'Where are they all now?'
'Some of them may have bettered themselves, I shouldn't wonder,' said Homily sharply. 'Times have changed in the whole house. Pickings aren't what they were. There were those that went, you remember, when they dug a trench for the gas-pipe. Over the fields, and through the wood, and all. A kind of tunnel it gave them all the way to Leighton Buzzard.'
'And what did they find there?' said Pod unkindly. 'A mountain of coke!'

It is scarcely necessary, perhaps, to emphasise how much there is of Mary Norton in this passage. If I say that the overriding quality can only be called 'wit', I do not use the word to mean, simply, sharp observation, but to characterise the way in which Mary Norton's presentation of incident and experience also renders at once a sense of the conditioned nature of life and of its possibilities. (Of course, it is in this sense that wit is characteristic of Jane Austen.)

The term 'wit' also picks up that teasing quality in the handling of the story which I mentioned earlier. Mary Norton is at great pains to confuse the reader as to the status of the narrative–whether it is a story made up by one or more of the 'characters' (Mrs May, her brother, Tom Goodenough, 'Kate') or whether it is a 'real' story in which those characters participate. So far as I know Mary Norton is the only contemporary writer for children to play with the idea of fiction in this way–so that the work becomes something of a metaphysical game. If she is indeed of the 'right', she is in this remarkably modern and radical. In works of the nineteenth-century tradition, to which all children's writers except Lewis Carroll and Mary Norton appear to belong, words are offered as equivalent to a 'reality' which is given. Many modern artists, however, invite us to consider the act of creation *in* the work of art. The world in the work is seen as created, not given. Herein lies the liberating and radical effect of successful modern art. If the world is made, not given, it is also 'potential' and changeable. Wit is the quality which renders this awareness.

These terms enable us to see in another way why the creative imagination is a central preoccupation of Mary Norton's. Her minor works focus the problem with peculiar sharpness. *Paul's Tale*, a short story, is truly a *jeu d'esprit*. Paul's Aunt attempts to tell him a not very convincing fairy-tale. By way of diversion Paul suggests a 'real' story about a little man 'as high... as that candlestick on the mantelshelf, but without the candle'. By supplying more and more circumstantial details about the little man, Paul goes on to trap his Aunt (and the reader) into 'believing' in him–thus demonstrating what he means 'about stories being real'. This display of virtuosity gives an effect of hollowness, as if, crudely speaking, the author were to say: 'I can make you believe any old story. So what?' In other words the author's imaginative talent itself is subject to the question, 'What, ultimately, for?' Why tell yet another story? Another story, for instance, like *Poor Stainless*, which was actually written (out of kindness, evidently) for *The Eleanor Farjeon Book*, in 1966, a story which entirely lacks the pressure of that self-questioning, and, attempting to pass itself off in the nineteenth-century manner (the word is the thing), paradoxically fails to convince.

With persistent logic, in her most recent book, *Are All the Giants Dead?*, Mary Norton actually attempts to confront head-on the question 'What is it to be a writer of children's books in our time?' She sets out on a witty and self-reflective exploration of the whole corpus of fairy-tales. An important aspect of Mary Norton's wit is her superbly controlled use of, and movement between, different modes and conventions. In its opening pages *Are All the*

Giants Dead? not only wittily exposes to each other the conventions of fairy-tale and realistic novel, but focuses the theme in the figure of Mildred, who, as journalist *and* magician, is a surrogate figure for the children's writer who is working that exposure. Meanwhile the boy in the story, James, would in any case prefer science fiction. So what are these fictions for? But the book is an intensely interesting failure. The wit vanishes half-way through and the remainder of the book becomes a mere mechanical working out of the purely narrative complications—in the same wooden manner as we find in *Poor Stainless*. When the writing loses touch with the animating question—'What am I writing for?'—it becomes literally pointless.

The development of Mary Norton's work as far as the impasse reached in *Are All the Giants Dead?* gives us a phenomenon of very considerable cultural significance. Why are the energising questions of the first half of the book apparently beyond living resolution? To begin to deal with that enquiry is to ask such questions as—What are *our* fictions worth? What ends do our imaginations serve? Why continue to reproduce *our* reality? How can our world be renewed? Mary Norton may not have achieved the miracle of answering these questions, but to have given us a living sense of what is at issue constitutes something other than retreat.

(1976)

Books by Mary Norton

Bedknob and Broomstick Dent, 1957. (First published separately as *The Magic Bedknob* (1945) and *Bonfires and Broomsticks* (1947))
The Borrowers Dent, 1952 (Carnegie Medal)
The Borrowers Afield Dent, 1955
The Borrowers Afloat Dent, 1959
The Borrowers Aloft Dent, 1961
Poor Stainless Dent 1971
Are All the Giants Dead? Dent, 1975
Paul's Tale appeared in *A Golden Land*, edited by James Reeves, Constable, 1958

Philippa Pearce

by

BRIAN JACKSON

OURS IS the golden age of children's literature. It took a thousand years to hammer out the folk and fairy tales. It took two full centuries to give us a small shelf of classics which, like *Gulliver's Travels*, were hungrily drawn into children's culture. Or which, like *Alice*, prettily married an adult's disintegrating vision to a child's kaleidoscopic sense of life's logics and meanings. Or which, like *Treasure Island* or *Kidnapped*, extended the adult novel downwards until it caught and mirrored back the adolescent's dawning perception of the ambiguities, the disappearing black and white of life. The quarrel between Davie and Alan, or Jim Hawkin's conflicting sense of Long John Silver's malice and radiance, are the entry to the adult novel and to adult life.

By and large, the children's classics of the eighteenth and nineteenth centuries tell us something of the unsatisfied needs of the child who read books –what pains they would go to, to quarry out their fiction. Or they show us adults on strange subterranean travels posing their problems via children. Or they represent the threshold of the novel proper.

I suppose the Edwardians–J M Barrie, A A Milne, Kenneth Grahame–are the outstanding example of adults pretending to write for children, when they are really writing for other adults. Of course they do this with an intermittent brilliance that redeems the sometimes cloying sweetness of their art. And, of course, there are writers–like E Nesbit–who would require a quite different account.

Nevertheless, it does not seem surprising that the classics of the past (and too often they still constitute *the* children's classics) have lost so much relative ground with children over the last thirty years. I suppose that what has happened is first of all the creation of a universal child public. The overwhelming majority of children can, for the first time, read for pleasure. And the overwhelming majority are different from the readers (or the read-to) of the past in that they are the children of the common man and not of the middle-class nursery. Secondly, it is certainly true that we are by far the most child-centred society that any civilisation has created. Perhaps it was the eighteenth century which really discovered childhood, and the nineteenth which conspired to treasure it as a special state. But it is this century which has revealed its breadth and richness. To Swift, children were miniature adults–as they are in eighteenth-century paintings. To Carroll, or later Barrie, they were ourselves during a fragile, transient stage of innocence. But what can *we* say except that children are children? We expect them to live, and not die; to be slowly and carefully educated, not tossed into child labour. We expect them to have their special tastes in food, dress, amusement. They are for the first time a market to some, an audience to others. And we see them, of course, through eyes imperceptibly altered by Freud.

Perhaps this goes some way to explaining why it was possible for ours to be the golden age of children's literature–and why the old classics begin to settle into a different perspective. The great writers of our time–like Meindert DeJong, Rosemary Sutcliff, René Guillot–have a sense of the child's inward life, of the normalities of growing up, and an ease and naturalness in their address to children, which is quite fresh.

Unfortunately, it is probably true that most adults interested in books have little awareness of what is transient or abiding in the crammed shelves of the children's libraries (consider the fact that there *are* children's libraries). And naturally they are guided by the books that impressed their own childhood, before the great creative explosion took place. In this note I'd like to give some account of Philippa Pearce. Not because she is one of the greatest. Or not yet. But because her achievement, wonderful enough in itself, is representative of how (without forsaking the adult note) a truly gifted writer can now write directly for the child, and for the ordinary child, in a way seldom achieved before.

Philippa Pearce published her first novel, *Minnow on the Say*, in 1955. In plain lucid prose, wholly accessible to a child between eight and twelve, she tells the story of two boys, their canoe and their hunt for an Elizabethan treasure hidden and lost 'over the water'. The tale has the hypnotic craftsmanship of a first-class detective story. And as the story winds its fascinating course, the book engages the reader even more deeply in the lovely re-creation of a boy's life in a small East Anglian village. In doing so, it brings back many childhoods–how tall the walls are, how beckoning the holes in fences, how the fingers reach to caress the dents and bulges in old stonework or to savour the speed and weight and coolness of dripping water or running streams. It spills over with a child's geography, places that only a child would know–like the fallen tree bridge over the river, from where they observe the punters below; or views that a child might specially sense, like the roof-well on Adam's house:

The door opened on to something quite different: a kind of minute courtyard, floored with lead and with the slopes of the slate-roofing for its four walls. It was a well in the middle of the roof, of the kind that is quite often found in old houses. From below roof-level, one would never have suspected its existence. It made a charming secret retreat, airy and sunny; it was a perfect hiding-place.

Together they peered over the ridge, looking outwards and downwards–far–far. Codlings' was an exceptionally high-built house–probably the highest building in Great Barley, not counting the church. It gave a view over roof-tops and tree-tops, and far out over the countryside. The boys could see the River Say winding away towards the bridge at Little Barley; they could see the railway line, and the place where it crossed the little iron bridge over the old channel of the Say–they watched a train pass over, on its way to London; they watched its smoke drift with the wind over the water-meadows–drift and dissolve.

'I say!' said David, awed. 'You're lucky to have a roof like this, Adam!'

It is, if you like, a very conservative book. Children are expected to be polite to adults, to make things–scraping and varnishing their canoe–not to destroy. There are all the tiny ceremonies of inviting friends to tea, or calling on strangers. Pocket-money is earned and carefully counted, and very neatly you pick up the nuances of children and adults observing the codes:

David was not yet in despair. 'Mr Ellum pays me my newspaper money at the end of this month; perhaps he'd pay me for as much delivery as I've done so far.'

Mr Ellum, when the difficulty had been twice explained to him, agreed to the arrangement David suggested. The money from Mr Ellum, together with what very little Adam and David already had, was given to Mr Moss on one of his trips to Castleford. He visited the boat-yards in his dinner-hour and brought back to David the container quite filled.

'I say,' said Adam, when he saw it, 'that's more than I expected for the money.'

'Is it?' said David, puzzled. 'My father just said, "Here's your varnish." It's the right kind, I know.'

'Anyway,' said Adam, 'we've so much, we ought to be able to put the second coat on outside, and one inside as well.'

Of course, the boys–being boys–are sometimes rude and destructive, thoughtlessly or at moments of stress. There is the moment when Adam, obsessed by the treasure, suspects treasure under the lovely pinky-yellow rose bush that stands by itself in the garden:

Adam handed the garden-fork to David. 'Hold that,' he said. He passed quickly indoors; he was back again in a minute.

'She's busy in the kitchen,' he said. 'It's all clear.' He took the fork from David and, with speed and force, drove the prongs in at the foot of the rose-tree.

'Here!' cried David, bewildered and horrified. 'Adam!'

'I told you,' Adam gasped, as he dug away. 'It's a single rose–the only single rose in the garden.'

David watched in a state of dazed apprehension: he seemed to be in a waking nightmare. It was almost a relief when the inevitable spectator appeared: Squeak Wilson came, trundling a wheelbarrow and whistling. He stopped both, when he saw Adam and what he was doing. For once, Squeak was too appalled to be frightened for himself. 'That's the Empress of Chiny you're at there!' he shrilled. Adam worked on, paying no attention.

'That's your grandpa's Empress of Chiny rose! He'd be that upset!'

Adam turned his head. 'Go away and be quiet!'

Squeak left his wheelbarrow, and went away, but he could not have obeyed the rest of Adam's order. In a few minutes, Miss Codling appeared at the garden-door, with Squeak peering out from behind her.

'Adam!' she shouted—no, she screamed it, rather.

Adam had only a little more digging to do, and he did not stop now. David could see the sweat rolling off his cheeks like tears; his muscles flowed and knotted and flowed again; the fork thrust and heaved and whirled up and away, like a gleaming, deadly instrument of war.

Miss Codling screamed again, and set off across the lawn towards Adam. She reached him at the exact moment that the fork completed its work: it had made a deep, raw hole, empty now of any rose-tree roots, and empty, too, of anything else. There was no treasure.

Without being in the slightest moralistic, the book has the rare capacity to create goodness, to make the decencies of life ring true.

Her effects come through her art; her negatives—'a deep, raw hole, empty now of any rose-tree roots'—imply her positives.

And yet there is more; already at least a pre-echo of the Philippa Pearce music, that note of controlled poignancy that is to make *Tom's Midnight Garden* a classic of its literature. You hear something of it with Squeak's tipsy bicycle ride past the bewildered David:

A voice somewhere down the drive began singing in queer, thin tones that might have come from another world. David felt almost frightened, until he saw that the singer was Squeak Wilson going home, the capacious basket of his tricycle piled high, as usual. He paid no attention to David even when he drew level with him. Now, David could hear the words of his little song:

'Heigh-ho!

Heigh-ho!

Heigh-ho! Sweet summer!'

All the sweet summers that David had ever known came drifting into his mind, and last came this one—best of them all, that he had shared with Adam. He heard the swish of the 'Minnow' as they paddled her along the Say; he saw again the moonlight silvering the water-meadows by Jonathan Codling's bridge; he smelt—yes, he really smelt—the delicious scents that follow in their order the summer through—only these were mixed together all at once—hawthorn and cowslips in the meadows; in the garden, apple-mint and clary, honeysuckle and roses. A wave of summer sweetness moved over David as Squeak passed, singing.

I could not imagine J M Barrie or Kenneth Grahame or A A Milne striking that note, without indulging its plangency. But here the flit of the mind backwards is given to the child–the open adult note is controlled–and the prose implies the cyclic promise of summer, not unstoppable regret for years gone by. How fine too the modulation in the next paragraph to plainer vision and quiet humour:

They did not greet each other–Squeak did not seem even to see David. He appeared, as David reported later to Miss Codling, to be, if anything, more cheerful than usual. The only sign of what was to come was, perhaps, in the wavering course he steered up the drive on his tricycle. He did not seem quite in control of it; on the other hand, he certainly did not seem to care.

Tom's Midnight Garden itself was published in 1958. A small boy at the thirteenth hour, between sleeping and waking, ventures downstairs to find that the backyard of their converted flats has slipped into its older self as a Victorian garden. Listen how clearly the characteristic music sounds now: the precision of place, the child geography, the deep-sunk sense of dream all marvellously fused together:

The green of the garden was greyed over with dew; indeed, all its colours were gone until the touch of sunrise. The air was still, and the tree-shapes crouched down upon themselves. One bird spoke; and there was a movement when an awkward parcel of feathers dislodged itself from the tall fir-tree at the corner of the lawn, seemed for a second to fall and then at once was swept up and along, outspread on a wind that never blew, to another, farther tree: an owl. It wore the ruffled, dazed appearance of one who has been up all night.
Tom began to walk round the garden, on tiptoe. At first he took the outermost paths, gravelled and box-edged, intending to map for himself their farthest extent. Then he broke away impatiently on a cross-path. It tunnelled through the gloom of yew-trees arching overhead from one side, and hazel nut stubs from the other: ahead with a grey-green triangle of light where the path must come out into the open again. Underfoot the earth was soft with the humus of last year's rotted leaves. As he slipped along, like a ghost, Tom noticed, through gaps in the yew-trees on his right, the flick of a lighter colour than the yew; dark–light–dark–light–dark...The lighter colour, he realised, was the back of the house that he was glimpsing, and he must be passing behind the line of yew-trees that faced it across the lawn.

Again the tale has the same breathless, detective pull. The garden fills with people, and one, Hatty, can see him. 'She had made this garden a kind of kingdom' and night after night they explore it together:

...a leafy crevice between a wall and a tree-trunk, where a small human body could just wedge itself; a hollowed-out centre to a box-bush, and a run leading to it–like the run made in the hedge by the meadow; a wigwam shelter made by a rearrangement of the bean-sticks that Abel had left leaning against the side of the heating-house; a series of hiding-holes behind the fronds of the great ferns that grew along the side of the greenhouse; a feathery green tunnel between the asparagus ridges. She showed Tom how to hide from a search simply by standing behind the trunk of the big fir-tree: you had to listen intently and move exactly—and noiselessly, of course—so that the trunk was always between yourself and the searcher.

But in the garden—even there—time moves too, and Hatty grows older. Who, once having read them, can forget the chapters when boy and young woman skate up the river to Ely?

For it is in these final sections that the art transcends itself. Through scenes of haunting and sometimes painful beauty, Tom perceives that the old woman in the upstairs flat was once a child like Hatty, and that age and life will make Hatty an old woman like her: 'he began to notice, again and again, a gesture, a tone of voice, a way of laughing that reminded him of the little girl in the garden.' It is, if you like, one of the ordinary insights of life; but one, perhaps, we most easily slurr over (as when politicians talk of 'old-age pensioners' as if they were a separate breed of human animal). Philippa Pearce makes you find it, feel it—and for her child audience it is perhaps the first uncovering:

Afterwards, Aunt Gwen tried to describe to her husband that second parting between them. 'He ran up to her, and they hugged each other as if they had known each other for years and years, instead of only having met for the first time this morning. There was something else, too, Alan, although I know you'll say it sounds even more absurd...Of course, Mrs Bartholomew's such a shrunken little old woman, she's hardly bigger than Tom, anyway: but, you know, he put his arms right round her and he hugged her good-bye as if she were a little girl.'

In 1962 came *A Dog So Small*. Again it has the clean narrative pull, the delicious quiet humour, an essential inwardness as it unfolds his world through a boy's eyes. Ben Blewitt longs for a tiny dog, a chihuahua: 'a dog so small you can only see it with your eyes shut', he says in a moment of despair as he begins to create a fantasy dog behind his closed eyes. The chapters where boy and puppies play in the pig sty are marvellously done:

They went to see Tilly's puppies. She did not want them to go; but, if they were going, she knew that her duty was to go too, and to go ahead. She went briskly but with a waddle, being incommoded by the swinging heaviness of the milk for her puppies.
The sty had once belonged to some pigs, but was now perfectly clean, with plenty of fresh straw on the concrete floor and a special lamp suspended low from one corner of the roof to give a gentle heat. Beneath this the puppies had all crawled and crowded together, and lay sleeping, a large, thick, sleek blob of multiple puppy-life.

And so too is the closing sequence as dusk falls on Hampstead Heath. It is a very fine book, and yet–coming where it does in her work–it is something of a pendant, a detour. So much is there, but not the music. The theme of obsession (which, of course, informed the treasure hunt in *Minnow on the Say*) now dominates and fills the gap. There is something of the psychological study about it, and–ever so slightly–the eye slips off the child audience. Characteristically, she no longer relies wholly on her art to do its own work, but–again, ever so slightly–tops up the insights with glimpses of *sententiae*: 'He saw that if you didn't have the possible things, you had nothing.' 'Granny shaded her eyes, looking after them. "People get their heart's desire," she said, "and then they have to begin to learn how to live with it".'

It seemed at that stage that either *Tom's Midnight Garden* had exhausted the more elusive and precious vein, or that having hit such brilliant moments the writer was reluctant to make the even more demanding commitment to her talents that was perhaps required.

In the event, she felt her way out of the situation with cautious instinct. Her book *The Children of the House* was published in 1968. The book was originally drafted by Brian Fairfax-Lucy, as a tale for adults. Philippa Pearce worked on the existing draft and, as the introductory note says, 'made it one that can be enjoyed and understood by children'. She did a good deal more than that. She made it a classic. The setting could be that of one of the Victorian or Edwardian writers. Four children grow up in a grand country house. Long corridors, candles to bed, lessons in the 'schoolroom', tea in the nursery, ha-has and pineapple houses, outlying tenant-farms and long gallops:

'Hugh,' said his father, 'you will ride this morning.'
'Yes, Papa.'
'But as I shall be busy with papers, you will ride with William.' The clouds rolled back from Hugh's morning: ride with *William!*
Their mother took over now. 'This afternoon Papa and I have to attend a meeting. I want you all to take a rice-pudding to old Mrs Higgs in the village. You can go in the pony-trap–Laura had better drive. After that, you may play in the garden.'

It is a grand loveless childhood, with the four children twined together in mutual and sustaining affection. The servants bring them up, and our images of fathering and mothering come when Elsie the maid or Walter the butler, for a moment, tend the children. The formal parents are defined by their absence:

After tea Walter wanted to buy some tobacco in the village, and took Margaret with him. She held his hand all the way, and he gave her twopence to spend on chocolate. Then he saw her back into the park, saying, 'This is my great chance for a drink and a chat in the pub, you know.' Sir Robert disapproved of his staff visiting public houses.

Margaret ran most of the way back across the park, because she was afraid of its getting dark and because she wanted to show Elsie her chocolate. But when she reached the kitchen, Elsie was out; so she went up to the schoolroom. All was quiet; there was nothing to do, nobody to talk to. She watched out of the window until outside grew dark. Then she turned up the lamp, and waited with the door open, for her supper. As she sat, the schoolroom seemed to get larger and the passage outside wider and longer, like a dark street in a town. Then the between-maid came with her supper of soup and a cake. 'And Alice says, Go to bed when you have finished, and she will be up later.'

What takes it out of the standard Victorian mould (as it does E Nesbit) is a refusal to identify with the assumptions and aspirations of the upper-class home–the sense of the house through the servants' eyes, of the eldest daughter denied a useful education, of the old men combing the bins, or the ironic stonebreaker on the roadside:

'Anyway,' said Laura, looking sideways at Hugh, 'you're doing a very useful job now, I suppose.'
'Oh, yes.' He made the same throaty sound. 'I'm glad to think that I'm making the stones ready to fill the pot-holes in the road, so that the carriages won't bump about so much. That's bad for the springs of the carriages and for the coachmen and the horses and the fine gentry that ride in the carriages.' He seemed to be staring at them, but they could not see his eyes properly behind the glasses.
'We must be going on, I'm afraid,' said Tom.

Compared with her previous books–and perhaps because of the curious joint authorship–it takes some chapters before the vision becomes as freed from its setting as this. And it nowhere has the potent narrative thread.

But it has the music. The beautiful, piercing sense of childhood swept along–and overswept–in the stream of time. The art is superb. The ordinary incidents of childhood–boiling a moorhen's egg, a forbidden hair-clipping, finding a half-crown–lap quietly in the reader's mind: months and years imperceptibly vanish at each chapter's end.

So apt and unforced is the second half that you may not realise how it is all building up inside you until the marvellous final section, the *adieu*. There is something almost Chekov-like in those last dozen pages. For one splendid stretch she again meets and tops the great Victorians in their own arbour.

I do not think any age previous to ours could have so brought out Philippa Pearce's talent. Her clean, plain prose opens up her books to any child who reads at all easily. I fear that isn't at all true of many revered classics of the past. Her work brims with life, and with life decent, positive, ongoing. Again one wonders if a critical look at some of our Edwardian inheritance might find that this was precisely what some of them lacked. She writes, mostly, to and for the child: not through the child to other adults.

In many ways I feel very puzzled by the great outburst of first-class children's books this last thirty years. It is not too hard to see the social conditions that underpin it. And yet in all previous periods which have given us children's classics, there has been a sturdy adult literature. The folk and fairy tales are often that very literature, slipping, over a thousand years, from the oral world of men and women to the pages of children's books. *Gulliver's Travels* or *Robinson Crusoe* in the eighteenth century, *Treasure Island* or *Bevis* in the nineteenth, are extensions of the flourishing adult novel, and Swift, Defoe, Stevenson, Jefferies, are writers for adults, accidentally or *en passant* entering the children's field. Equally, Lewis Carroll or E Nesbit may, if you like, be among the earlier writers who specialised with distinction in children's work. Yet there is never any doubt that they are supported by the flourishing adult novel. And at any rate, it is *there*. Yet it isn't now. At least, I don't think so. And children's writing is a large and apparently self-contained *genre*, as it never was before. It is independent of the current adult novel. On the face of it you wouldn't therefore expect its burgeoning richness. Could it be, ironically, that precisely because the adult novel is so weak in this country, some talents have been drawn into the children's field and flourished (as others have been drawn into science fiction, and perished)?

It is hard to puzzle out. But a writer like Philippa Pearce, quite apart from the significance of her books, indicates how fertile and accommodating this ground has been. Though it is indeed a golden age which could think of her still mint genius as silver.

(1970)

Books by Philippa Pearce

Fiction

Minnow on the Say OUP, 1955
Tom's Midnight Garden OUP, 1958 (Carnegie Medal)
Mrs Cockle's Cat Longman, 1961
A Dog So Small Longman, 1962
The Strange Sunflower Nelson, 1966
The Children of the House (with Brian Fairfax-Lucy) Longman, 1968
The Elm Street Lot BBC Publications, 1969
The Squirrel Wife Longman, 1971
Beauty and the Beast Longman, 1972
What the Neighbours Did and Other Stories Longman, 1972

Anthology

Stories from Hans Andersen Collins, 1972

Non-Fiction

From Inside Scotland Yard (with Harold Scott) André Deutsch, 1963

K M Peyton

by

DENNIS BUTTS

IN A review of some historical novels for children, Leon Garfield, writing in *The Guardian*, suggested that historical novels seem to fall into two distinct categories, which he called the *doglike* and the *catlike*. 'The doglike,' he said with characteristic wit, 'is when the author deliberately looks back and makes his characters subordinate to his history. Generally such books are large, a shade ponderous, but helpful; and they never mind being put down in the middle...The catlike category is when the author looks not back but about him and his history is subordinate to his characters. These books tend to be smaller, sleeker, and more self-contained. They don't aim to be particularly helpful, but once picked up, they grip rather more and fiercely resist being put down.'

Though this is a useful way of starting to think about historical writers like Cynthia Harnett or Leon Garfield himself for that matter, it is only a starting-point, partly because while some writers seem to fit fairly easily into one category or the other, for other writers the dividing-line is harder to find (is Gillian Avery doglike or catlike?) and others seem to fit into both categories or neither.

As George Lukacs has shown, the historical novel arose at the beginning of the nineteenth century at about the time of Napoleon's collapse, when writers first became aware of the social and human motives which led men to think and act in the ways they did, and were able to identify these movements in terms of individual destinies. Once the *genre* of the historical novel had been established, and in children's literature it was probably with Marryat's *Children of the New Forest* in 1847, writers were able to use it to explore deeply personal themes, to recreate a convincing picture of the past, and to examine the ways in which the values of the past have led to the values of the present.

The best historical novelists have tended to integrate successfully all these aims in the same way as the best realistic novelists are convincing both psychologically and sociologically. 'What matters therefore in the historical novel,' to quote Lukacs directly, 'is not the retelling of great historical events, but the poetic awakening of the people who figured in these events...and it is a law of literary portrayal which first appears paradoxical, but then quite obvious, that in order to bring out these social and human origins of behaviour, the outwardly insignificant events, the smaller (from without) relationships are better suited than the great dramas of world history.' (*The Historical Novel.*)

Kathleen Peyton is more than a historical novelist, and has written interestingly of contemporary life, particularly in her remarkable *Pennington's Seventeenth Summer*. But the majority of the books published since 1963 have been set in the past, where, despite the success of *Windfall* and *The Maplin Bird*, there is little doubt that her most impressive achievement is to be found in the *Flambards* trilogy, consisting of *Flambards, The Edge of the Cloud*, and *Flambards in Summer*, all available in Oxford paperbacks.

Any summary of these stories, each of which can be read quite separately by the way, though it is obviously best to read them in their published order, is bound to risk doing the books a disservice from the danger of over-emphasising their richly romantic structure–they do have young orphans, handsome cousins, ponies, and a passionate elopement; but the risk is worth taking, partly because it is these elements which help to make the books popular with adolescents,* and also because these elements, Lukacs' 'outwardly insignificant events', are beautifully integrated by Mrs Peyton into a serious and sustained view both of adolescence and historical movement. The opening paragraphs of *Flambards*, for example, suggest a whole way of life through the evocative images of the fox-hunt across the autumn meadows. But the presence of another and contrasting way of life, creating a source of major tension within the novel, is deftly suggested by the presence of the hedger standing sardonically by.

Christina is twelve when the first book opens. She is an orphan brought up by a series of maiden-aunts, and will inherit a lot of money when she comes of age. Though the absence of parents makes her more romantic, it does also have the significant effect of leaving her without roots, of never quite knowing where she belongs socially. Her Uncle Russell invites her to stay with him at his great country-house called Flambards, because he has an eye to his elder son Mark's marrying her (and her money) when they are older. It is a peculiar household, run by a maid and a housekeeper, and dominated by Uncle Russell and Mark, both of whom are passionately fond of riding and hunting. Although the old man has been crippled in a riding accident and drinks a lot to deaden the pain, he and his son are obsessed by horses and riding to the exclusion of everything else. They both bully the

* *Flambards* was the fifth most popular novel chosen by 900 teenagers in a survey published in *The Observer* in April, 1971, falling below *The Hobbit* and *Wuthering Heights* but above *The Owl Service* and *Treasure Island*.

younger son, Will, into riding as well, which he hates, for he is keener on cars and aeroplanes, and they soon persuade Christina to learn to ride though she enjoys it.

As an example of Mrs Peyton's power to handle a dramatic situation in purely human terms, it is worth looking at the scene where Christina discovers that Will, who has broken his leg in a riding accident, is deliberately walking on it at night in order to prevent the bones knitting properly:

'Whatever are you doing?' she hissed. 'Are you mad?'
She set the candle down and went over to him, holding out her arms. His face was a greenish colour in the firelight, and pinched with pain, so that his eyes stood out as if twice their usual size, blazing with a defiant agony that put Christina at a complete loss.
'What are you doing? Here, hold me!'
For a moment she thought he was going to fall. He swayed, but half-turned away from her arms as if he would run from her if he could. He took a staggering pace on the stiff broken leg, half-cried out, and collapsed into the small chair in front of the fire.
'William! What are you trying to do? Do you want something? You only had to call me!'
Christina dropped down on her knees beside him, horrified by the ordeal he had inflicted on himself. His face was shining with sweat, and he moaned, twisting himself in the chair, turning his head away from her. Christina was frantic to help him.
'William! Don't–don't–!'
She remembered the brandy bottle downstairs in the dining-room, and got up and ran, holding up her night-dress. In her bare feet she sped down the stairs and across the hall to the well-used sideboard where Uncle Russell's bottles stood shoulder to shoulder. His empty glass was still there. She grabbed it and the brandy and ran back upstairs again. She remembered to shut the door, feeling that it was quite imperative that no one else should know what was going on.
'Here, drink this.'
She put her arm round William's shoulders and held the glass to his lips. William resisted, shrinking from her like a hunted rabbit, but Christina pushed the glass at him relentlessly.
'Here, you idiot! Or shall I fetch Mary?'
He drank the brandy at last, gasping and shuddering. Christina fetched a blanket from the bed and wrapped it round him. He sat huddled in the chair, his broken leg in its plaster stuck out into the hearth. Christina put another log on the fire. William stared at the flames, his face stiff with some private agony which Christina could not even guess at. It was no longer a physical pain; it was something outside the realm of Dr Porter altogether.
'Are you all right?'
'Oh, stop fussing,' he whispered angrily. 'You didn't have to interfere, did you?'
'But what were you doing?'

'You could see, couldn't you? Just walking about.'

'But *why*? However will your leg mend if you walk on it? You know what Dr Porter said. What were you trying to do?'

Even as she asked the question Christina realised what was in William's mind. In the set, stubborn expression on his face, and by his very silence, she read the answer.

It is difficult to say which is more impressive here, the vivid realisation of Will's self-inflicted physical ordeal, or the subtle rendering of his 'private agony', an anguish so great as to give him the courage to cripple his whole life deliberately rather than face becoming a more conventional coward. Just as remarkable, though, is Christina's sensitive but highly practical response to the situation, her attempts to help reinforced by the rhythms of the prose ('She remembered...and...sped...grabbed...'), until she is forced to face the appalling logic of Will's behaviour.

The nature of this unhappy household is made even clearer, for when a horse goes lame Uncle Russell orders it to be shot, and when Christina and the stable-boy Dick try to save the horse, Dick is sacked at a moment's notice. Because of his game leg Will is excused riding now, and spends all his time in the village with rich, eccentric Mr Dermot, who is building his own aeroplane. Though Christina enjoys some aspects of life at Flambards, particularly the grounds and the riding, she hates the arrogant brutality, and gradually becomes attracted to the younger brother Will, although she recognises that he is as obsessed with flying as his older brother is with horses. A great crisis ends the first book when Will crashes the plane on to the field where Mark is riding in a point-to-point, and is ordered from the house. Christina realises that she is in love with him–she is now seventeen–so when he proposes to her and she realises how unbearable Flambards will be without him, she elopes with him.

They don't get married immediately though, on the advice of Aunt Grace, and decide to wait a while. Will obtains a job as an air mechanic and Christina a job in a hotel. Each weekend she goes down to Will's flying field and watches terrified as he gives people trips in an old plane. Not the least of Mrs Peyton's gifts is her ability to write convincingly of an adolescent's growing recognition of the complexities of adult life, as Christina struggles to come to terms with her love for a person whose frightening obsession she has to find the courage to endure. Finally, when Uncle Russell dies back at Flambards, they are free to marry and do so. It is 8 August, 1914, and Will soon joins the Royal Flying Corps.

He is killed in 1916 and so Christina is left widowed, but also rich. As Uncle Russell is dead and his elder son reported missing on active service, she returns to Flambards and tries to put the old decaying estate back on its feet. She hires two village boys to help her, and then traces Dick, the exstable-boy, whom she persuades to rejoin the estate now that he has been medically discharged from the army. A German prisoner-of-war is also taken on and gradually the land is reclaimed and turned into a working farm again. When Mark dramatically reappears–he had been in a Turkish prison-camp all the time–the old rivalry between him and Christina and Dick soon rises again, but Christina persuades him to sell Flambards to her. He leaves her on the point of marrying Dick, the former stable-boy, with the house which had stood 'unperturbed through eighty years of tiny human crises'.

It is clear that Kathleen Peyton's books deal with themes and interests of a rather wider and deeper kind than one finds in most children's books. The presence of death, the awareness of sexual love, the importance of money, give her novels an unusual texture for which their romantic structures provide a successful and accessible framework.

Even more remarkable perhaps is her moving and perceptive account of English social history over the first two decades of this century, describing society as it was, how it changed, and what the nature of the changes were. Mrs Peyton's particular focus, of course, is on the disappearance of a landed but under-capitalised gentry, whose traditions were such an inextricable mixture of grace and boorishness, and their replacement by a, on the whole, more democratic, more civilised, social class. Indeed in the anticipated marriage of Christina and Dick one sees Mrs Peyton looking even further into the future in a scene not unlike the conclusion of *Howards End*.

It is the triumph of Mrs Peyton's art that she evokes this sense of social transformation by means of a few richly-actualised symbols in a historical romance of highly popular elements. The horse-riding and Hunt Ball of the *ancien régime*, the free-and-easy social manners of the airfield, stand out as the two supreme images, of course, the one looking back, the other to the future. Not the least of Mrs Peyton's successes is the way in which, while she confines her characters to a particular family group, her use of resonances delicately suggests the whole social fabric beyond them, as when Christina's friend Dorothy becomes a nurse in the war, or when Christina visits Dick's mother's slum cottage in the village, or when a maid is sacked for expecting an illegitimate baby.

The most potent symbol of all is Christina herself, a young romantic heroine, orphaned, isolated in a house of strange men, an heiress, not afraid to elope with the man she loves, a girl who likes riding and wearing grand party dresses, and yet is sensitive and alert to all the experiences around her. Here, as an example of the way she is realised both as a growing girl with emotional problems and as a filter of the social processes, we see her at the age of fifteen. She is just beginning to notice that Dick, the stable-boy, no longer treats her quite so freely when they are out riding. The 'barrier' that is coming between them is both social and sexual, of course:

Dick noticed her new habit too; she could tell by the way his eyes did not look, after the first flare of surprise.
She laughed and said, 'Don't you think I look smart, Dick? I'm as smart as Drummer now.'
'Why, yes, miss. You're a right pair.' He smiled, flushing slightly. He did not chat any more–as he once had when they had ridden through the fields together. Christina had noticed, gradually, that he no longer started conversations nor passed remarks, but only replied to her own observations. He had withdrawn, and she knew it was because of the convention that she had discussed with William. He treated her with more respect. A small part of Christina was flattered by this, but a larger, more logical part was grieved. She had wanted Dick to go on being a friend, as he had been when he had taught her to ride, but now the barrier between them was preventing it. What William had said, although she had laughed at him, had stuck in her mind, but Christina saw no way of bridging this gulf. She also felt that Dick was more anxious to keep it than she was herself, and she had a feeling that he wanted it in some way as a protection for himself, but as a protection from what she had no idea. When she was older she realised what it was, but when she was fifteen she had only vague feelings which she could never pin down, nor analyse. She always admired William for the way he was able to explain everything with his mathematician's logic, but she did not think that even William could explain what some of her feelings meant, nor even what they were. She thought that Aunt Grace would have been more helpful with her brisk, 'It's your age.'

So we see Christina standing at the meeting-point of so many tensions, uncertain, intelligent, loving–intensely human.

The subject-matter of the *Flambards* trilogy, together with its central heroine, suggest that it is likely to be especially appreciated by girl readers in the twelve to sixteen age range, but *The Observer* survey already referred to shows that it is more widely popular, and when I read it with a mixed third-year class in a comprehensive school, the boys seemed to enjoy it equally with the girls. Elsewhere, in *Windfall* or *Thunder in the Sky*, for example, the heroes are fairly tough teenage boys, which suggests a possible reading interest there.

But though Mrs Peyton's books make no linguistic concessions to younger readers, they do seem to be enjoyed by them sometimes, though this is more likely to be true of two of her contemporary novels, *The Plan for Birdsmarsh* and *Fly-by-Night*, the latter being particularly enjoyed by my nine-year-old daughter. Written as a diversion in the middle of the work on *Flambards*, it is an intelligently conceived pony story which explores the real problems that would face an eleven-year-old girl who wants to keep a pony and lives on a housing-estate. *The Plan for Birdsmarsh*, on the other hand, deals more dramatically with an older boy's attempts to prevent the coastal area where he lives being ruined by plans to build a marina there. Though the plot also involves some industrial spies who try to steal the plans for an exposure suit from the hero's brother, it is the boy's concern for his home which is really effective.

Whether the stories focus on girls or boys, and deal with contemporary events or the past, however, they nearly always deal with teenage children under pressure. Often deprived of parental help, like Christina of *Flambards* or Matt of *Windfall*, the central characters are put to the test of challenging circumstance, and in the process grow a little. Penn, the secondary school drop-out of *Pennington's Seventeenth Summer*, does have parents, but, despite their good intentions, they are as baffled by the conventions of middle-class society as he is. Lashing out in his frustrations, Penn gets into all kinds of trouble, refusing to follow his school's rules, letting a car's tyres down, and fighting on the sea-front, before he achieves a sense of fulfilment which is not anti-social. Despite the flaws in this extremely ambitious book, Penn does succeed in retaining the reader's sympathy, I think, and in the process makes us feel that there is a life here which adults may be in danger of misunderstanding. This is the funniest of all Mrs Peyton's books, and once again, as with *Flambards*, reveals the connections between the lives of individual characters and the larger society of which they are a part and a mirror. Though Kathleen Peyton's most striking achievements to date have been in the realms of the historical novel, books like *The Plan for Birdsmarsh* and *Pennington's Seventeenth Summer* cannot be overlooked, and one can only speculate upon the future of this very talented writer.

(1972)

Postscript

Since 1972 Kathleen Peyton has completed two more books about Pennington, written a highly competent pony story, *The Team*, and produced what is arguably her best novel to date, *A Pattern of Roses*.

The Pennington books, for all their considerable faults, still seem to me to represent a remarkable achievement. Overloaded with incidents, exaggerated, and often sentimental, they still make a brave attempt to get inside the mind of a sixteen-year-old drop-out.

Pennington's world is that of harsh circumstance, controlled by crude if occasionally well-meaning parents, against the background of what is to him a meaningless bourgeois society, administered by bullies and petty tyrants. Not surprisingly he reacts in boorish and anti-social ways, in themselves alienated and alienating. An eleven-plus reject, he gets his pleasures from beer, messing about in the water, and from violent horse-play.

Even when he is not responsible, he is usually blamed for what goes wrong, for a sudden outburst of violence, or for a Jaguar that has obscenities painted on it. Because authority is suspicious and hostile, he is hostile too. But what is extraordinary is the way Penn never forfeits his independence or the reader's sympathy. At the very moment when we know exactly why his parents or teachers react in the way they do towards his behaviour–for it is probably the way we would react–his vitality, ingenuity, and integrity keep us on his side.

Despite his problems and outbursts, Penn finds a focus for his energies and an outlet for his unrealised ability in playing the piano. Through the presence of two obsessive but sympathetic teachers, he finds himself forced to practise hard and regularly. He wins a piano competition in the first novel, gives a successful concert performance in the second, and begins a career as a professional musician in the third. During this time he has spent nine months in prison, but has learnt to control his violent energy and channel it to some extent into the creation of music.

There is an imbalance in the novels between their outer structure which is occasionally unconvincing–Penn's successes come all too quickly–and their internal structure, which sympathetically reveals Penn's own uncertainties and the gradual discovery of his own identity. But this inner revelation is still a bold attempt to explore the combination of destructive violence and genuine creativity, which Penn's formal triumphs are meant to externalise.

The behaviour of adolescents under pressure, and the need to be true to one's own inner nature, are two themes which have recurred in Mrs Peyton's work, in both the *Flambards* and *Pennington* trilogies. They come together cogently with another of her themes, the influence of the past on the present, in *A Pattern of Roses*, so as to make this so far the most formally satisfying of all her books.

Tim Ingram, recovering from glandular fever, finds, hidden in the chimney of the old country cottage his parents have just bought, some drawings done by a boy with the same initials as himself. He then comes across the boy's tombstone in the village churchyard, and discovers he died a month short of his sixteenth birthday. Moved and intrigued by the situation, Tim tries to find out more about the life of this boy, Tom, whose presence comes to haunt him. Through his discoveries about the boy's life and death, Tim begins to understand the value of love and of independence, and so becomes decisively aware of his own predicament, with the pressures of ambitious parents and A-levels. And he rebels:

There was a responsibility to follow through one's own potential because it had been built up from all that had happened earlier. And in this argument, he felt he owed it more to Tom than to his father–Tom whose own potential had never stood a chance, its struggling stopped by some arbitrary fate.

Once again we see in the combination of incidents and characters how Mrs Peyton sensitively yet dramatically articulates her meaning. Even then she can surprise us. For it is May, the spinsterish and unattractive girl, who finally gets married while Netty, the pretty cousin, stays single. At the end, May tells Tim that there may be something even more important in life than achieving one's potential, and in this way challenges the major thrusts of the novel as a whole. In a letter to Tim about Tom's death years before, she says:

'I often thought of this particularly in respect of Tom. His was such a sweet nature that if he had lived I think perhaps he would have suffered more in many ways than he did by dying in the way God chose for him. His life though short was very happy, for he demanded very little and accepted what he had with a perfect spiritual grace. This I do not expect you as a young person today to understand, and whether in fact it is a good thing or not I would not like to say. I am only stating what I know was true.'

This seems to me to be dramatically appropriate writing of high quality, both disconcerting and profoundly sad.

DENNIS BUTTS

Books by K M Peyton

Sabre, the Horse from the Sea (under name Kathleen Herald) A and C Black, 1947
The Mandrake (under name Kathleen Herald) A and C Black, 1949
Crab the Roan (under name Kathleen Herald), A and C Black, 1953
North to Adventure Collins, 1959
Stormcock Meets Trouble Collins, 1961
The Hard Way Home Collins, 1962
Windfall OUP, 1963
Brownsea Silver Collins, 1964
The Maplin Bird OUP, 1964
The Plan for Birdsmarsh OUP, 1965
Thunder in the Sky OUP, 1966
Flambards OUP, 1967
Fly-By-Night OUP, 1968
The Edge of the Cloud OUP, 1969
Flambards in Summer OUP, 1969
Pennington's Seventeenth Summer OUP, 1970
The Beethoven Medal OUP, 1971
A Pattern of Roses OUP, 1972
Pennington's Heir OUP, 1973
The Team OUP, 1975

Spellbinding and Anthropology: The Work of Richard Adams and Ursula LeGuin

by

FRED INGLIS

SCIENCE, WE say, has disenchanted the universe. It is a commonplace of every romantic poet and novelist to drink confusion to a varied demonology: with Keats to Newton, with Blake to Locke and Voltaire and Nebuchadnezzar, with Dickens to Bentham, with Lawrence to Russell, with Leavis to Descartes and Hume. The programme of English romanticism, that great tradition which is the course of so much popular and cultural strength today, was written out against the roll-call of European philosophy.

Did Jesus teach doubt? Or did He
Give any lessons in Philosophy?

The romantic poets and their heirs, the Victorian novelists, set themselves more or less explicitly against the victors of the Enlightenment, the Empiricists, the Rationalists, the *Philosophes*, men of gigantic and world-changing stature who, for all that, are still not part of popular cultural mythology in the way that Wordsworth and Shelley are, or the Ancient Mariner and his dreadful barque, Dickens and Emily Brontë, Miss Havisham's over-populated wedding cake, and Heathcliff's brow and temples glistening with blood as he beats them against the impassive tree-trunk. These are the names and these the images of English romanticism; amongst its heirs now may intelligibly be said to be the best of present-day children's novelists. They stand, as I have suggested elsewhere,* in something of the same relation to the great romantics as do the schoolteachers and librarians who provide the grounds of their intellectual genesis. Emerging from the slightly stuffy, still air of that hygienic and liberal-thinking clerisy, children's novelists claim,

* In my *Ideology and the Imagination* Cambridge 1975.

of course, a larger sense of responsibility for and towards the 'living principle' of human creativity which it is the special and formal concern of education to cherish in our culture, but to cherish in the name of those free and individual spirits, the writers and artists. Writers, we allege, cannot be members of any institution–such membership would stunt and suffocate the freedom and individuality which on this account (Mozart and Bach notwithstanding) are the necessary grounds of creation. The strength of literature in English culture has lain in this strong individualism; when children's novelists have spoken to and from that spring of being, they have found a congruent and congenial frame of mind and spirit, of understanding and response. With Blake and Wordsworth, with Dickens and Lawrence, or at any rate with the works of these writers as they are to be found marked on the maps of English culture, the best children's writers have largely spoken to the private life of the sensibility. It is in our feelings that we are most ourselves: this is the datum of a new Kierkegaard, and these feelings are most vividly and, we hope, sincerely lived in our personal relationships. Hence the stuff of novels and poems is the texture of personal feelings as lived in and shaped by relationships.

It is, as I say, a powerful frame of mind. It serves, as frames of mind should, to fix what is significant and to confer stable value on all the inanely transient and fluid surfaces of experience. For all that so many of the writers, and the teachers formally entrusted with explaining and expounding the writers, collapse at times into self-pitying admiration of their own powerlessness and ineffectuality, the largely dissident tradition of Romantic individualism provides–to speak largely–one of two main frames of interpretation for a nation and its times. We may roughly diagrammatise these frames by marking them 'private' and 'public'; the tension between the two seems both to generate and to confer values in the lives of most people; when the tension is not maintained in the lives either of persons or groups, then the shape of their lives no longer makes sense, it loses meaning, as we say, it falls into rulelessness and namelessness, the anonymity which causes one version of suicide.*

Novels, then, are, in this simple classification, 'private'. One place in which the tension of private and public modes of thought becomes most visible is in the curriculum, whether at primary, secondary, or tertiary levels. Education, after all, devises and settles the rules for recognising and working a society's modes of thought, and within education the quarrels between arts and sciences ('is history a science?' 'is sociology one of the humanities?' 'is literary criticism a proper discipline?') serve to mark for the time being the

---

* It is relevant to say that it is only one version; Durkheim thought it was the only one, but he antedated the extermination camps of the mid-twentieth century, in which suicide became a brave way to *affirm* and retain meaning.

proper, needful boundaries between the forms of knowledge, between theory and experience. But the public realm, as we all acknowledge with more or less resentment, belongs to science. And since (let us say) Bacon, Galileo, and Descartes, science has meant the knowledge we can identify according to the criteria of regular classification, observable and lawful data, the difficult establishment of an objective and transferable calculus. The triumph of the modes of thought ordered by these criteria has been vast and ungainsayable; its costs are less easily told. For our purposes, however, it is enough to say that novelists and poets have for 200 years or so tried to tell the costs and gainsay the triumph. What are interesting and important these days are the advances they and likeminded people have been making over the ground held for so long by traditional science. The frequency of the high tension between private and public modes of thought is varying strongly, and because this is so, the values signified by those modes of thought are changing also.

That is why I begin this essay with this potted history of ideas. We can hardly say what children will make of particular books; in the good phrase, we hope for the best. We ask ourselves, as teachers and as parents, what do I want my son, daughter, or pupil to have read, to have chosen to read, to enjoy reading, out of the books there are? (What will I *stop* them reading?) And we go on to make the books available in the way we hope will work. If we challenge ourselves to say what is it for a book to work, then, allowing for our unpleasant and sanctimonious preference for being right-minded rather than purposeful and effective, we shall ask of a book that it make it more possible for its reader to face our brave new world which hath such people in it, to face it and to face up to it with a set of values which are more absolute than expedient, but capable of living with the facts of relativism and change. And if, finally, this seems to make great demands on books for our children, let me say that the least but first of my demands is that a book give pleasure, but that pleasure is a formal term with many contents, and let me ask which parent who was not a monster would not demand of his child's book that it give pleasure in such a way as to celebrate what is good and true and beautiful.*

This is the large context within which I want to praise and blame Richard Adams and *Watership Down*, Ursula LeGuin and her trilogy, *A Wizard of Earthsea*, *Tombs of Atuan*, and *The Farthest Shore*. I take these books for a number of reasons. First, because they are famous, in the case of *Watership*

---

* For those scared at this point by Plato's ghost, I should say that celebration of that splendid trinity does *not* require that a writer deal only with healthy-minded subjects. What, of course, matters to us (as parents, teachers, and so forth) is *how* a writer treats of what is evil and loathsome: not *Chopper* and *Skinhead*–But louder sang that ghost, 'What then?'

Down unprecedentedly so, and they have won many prizes. They stand as major examples of books it is the point of this collection to criticise and explore, since they are warmly commended to children by teachers and librarians precisely because they carry and give life to values which that group of adults approve. Second and consequently, these books are interesting because they cross so many exclusive frontiers–Puffin and Penguin, historical novel and science fiction, left and right, commune and mews villa, high and pop culture; at a time when cultural life has made bureaucratic institutions out of the many mansions of the motherland's home of fiction, and when the floors of that house mark off so many neat stratifications (there is a killing rightness about the sociologist's metaphor, 'upward social mobility'), books which brim over the categories pose a challenge to think again about what matters to us and to others at a given time. In October 1974 alone, *Watership Down* sold 145,000 copies in the thirteen languages into which it is translated;* within three years of its Puffin publication, it had sold well over a million. Ursula LeGuin is a less spectacular and mysterious example of success, but she is a great name in the adult science fiction world; her Puffin trilogy has sold well over 20,000 copies a year since 1971, and (1976) is in its seventh printing.

Both authors provide a useful moment at which to look at the intersections of cult and culture, for the third ground and for my purposes centrally intellectual reasons for taking these books is that they represent bold, pedagogic attempts to draw together in a new synthesis the public and private frames of thought. Dr Adams and Miss LeGuin can hardly be said to have intentions in common: Dr Adam's creation is a loose and baggy monster; the difference between them is something like that of which Thomas Wolfe wrote to Scott Fitzgerald:

Just remember that although *Madame Bovary* in your opinion may be a great book, *Tristram Shandy* is indubitably a great book, and that it is great for quite different reasons. It is great because it *boils and pours*–for the *unselected* quality of its selection. You say that the great writer like Flaubert has consciously left out the stuff that Bill or Joe will come along presently and put in. Well, don't forget, Scott, that a great writer is not only a leaver-outer but also a putter-inner, and that Shakespeare and Cervantes and Dostoevsky were great putter-inners–greater putter-inners, in fact, than taker-outers and will be remembered for what they put in–remembered, I venture to say, as long as Monsieur Flaubert will be remembered for what he left out.†

Ursula LeGuin is much sparer and more austere, more artistic; although, for all that, her books smell sometimes intolerably of the study and the library

* 'Trend Setters: *Watership Down*' *The Guardian*, 6 August 1976.
† Reprinted in *The Crack-Up* New Directions (Scribners) 1954, p 314.

stack, and signally lack not only Adams' colour and eventfulness, but also a depth of characterisation in which the authoress is hardly interested, but which it is simply unimaginative and therefore morally unsympathetic to suppose her audience does not count on. What links the two writers and their work is the break they make with the conventions of the liberal novel for children, and the ways in which they render certain drastically changed features of the intellectual landscape, the contours of the mind, in such a way as to make children experience these changes for themselves.

One cannot doubt that both authors intend to strike this pedagogic note. Richard Adams, indeed, strikes it often clumsily–he can be clumsy in many ways, both when trying too hard and when not trying enough. From *Watership Down*:

When Marco Polo came at last to Cathay, seven hundred years ago, did he not feel–and did his heart not falter as he realised–that this great and splendid capital of an empire had had its being all the years of his life and far longer, and that he had been ignorant of it? That it was in need of nothing from him, from Venice, from Europe? That it was full of wonders beyond his understanding? That his arrival was a matter of no importance whatever? We know that he felt these things, and so has many a traveller in foreign parts who did not know what he was going to find. There is nothing that cuts you down to size like coming to some strange and marvellous place where no one even stops to notice that you stare about you.

That is a lapse into avuncularity of touch which occurs a number of times in the novel, although it is not unendearing, as with someone who has come to teaching during middle-age, benign but often awkward. Ursula LeGuin has both less and more to her. She doesn't put her foot down plonkingly in that way but she adopts an on occasions far more dauntingly high-minded tone, as here from *A Wizard of Earthsea*:

He looked for a spell of self-transformation, but being slow to read the runes yet and understanding little of what he read, he could not find what he sought. These books were very ancient, Ogion having them from his own master Heleth Farseer, and Heleth from his master the Mage of Perregal, and so back into the times of myth. Small and strange was the writing, overwritten and interlined by many hands, and all those hands were dust now.

It is this severity of approach, perfectly congruent as it is with something even starker to which she subjects her hero, which surely confirms her purpose. By the same token, Richard Adams has in a less inward way a point to press on when he writes. Again from *Watership Down*:

Rabbits, of course, have no idea of precise time or of punctuality. In this respect they are much the same as primitive people, who often take several days over assembling for some purpose and then several more to get started. Before such people can act together, a kind of telepathic feeling has to flow through them and ripen to the point when they all know that they are ready to begin.

There is more than a touch here, as elsewhere about Richard Adams, of a Sir James Frazer's bluff patronage–'these chappies have their own rummy way of doing things, can never quite follow them meself'–which sorts perfectly well with the glimpses we get of the red-bereted officer elsewhere, with his Sergeant-Major Bigwig, his Captain Holly, his 'Thus it fell to one of the rank-and-file to make a lucky find', and 'the injured doe...was clearly in a bad way'. But the same pages give us a different cue as well; they make the connection, certainly, with the anthropologists, but these are not merely the anthropologists hired by the nineteenth-century Empire to report on the peculiarities of colonial peoples. They have moved with the times which have dispersed that Empire, and they seek a moral account of the change, an account which will explain some of the varieties of human experience, its openness and closures. To do this, they have sought to enter alien minds and experience the world with the concepts and values of those minds.

It is at this point that the two modes of thought which I set earlier in diagrammatic opposition come into a common though necessarily blurred focus. For Adams is a novelist, and as such committed to the understanding and inhabitation of other frames of mind. Insofar as novels are the product of one tributary from the Enlightenment age, he is engaged upon the traditional Romantic enterprise of seeing how subjectivities work. But, as I say, there is a different anthropology astir as well, and insofar as Adams seeks systematically to render an alien perception of the world, he is very much engaged in the new science. *The New Science* was the title of Giambattista Vico's great work, now 270 years old; I mention it because of Isaiah Berlin's recent championing of Vico in the name of a new social science as it begins to push its way through the great dustheaps of computation which have piled themselves atop of human behaviour for so long. Vico, Berlin says, seeks for

yet another type of awareness, unlike *a priori* knowledge in that it is empirical, unlike deduction in that it yields new knowledge of facts, and unlike perception of the external world in that it informs us not merely of what exists or occurs, and in what spatial or temporal order, but also why what is, or occurs, is as it is, i.e. in some sense *per causas*. This species is self-knowledge: knowledge of activities of which we, the knowing subjects, are ourselves the authors, endowed with motives, purposes and a continuous social life, which we understand, as it were, from the inside...*

* Isaiah Berlin *Vico and Herder: Two Studies in the History of Ideas* Hogarth Press 1975, p 21-2.

What Berlin goes on to show is not so much 'self-knowledge', as the phrase is conventionally understood, as knowledge of others, and it is this technique of empathic interpretation which he seeks to commend to us as the life and truth-giving tendency of a new hermeneutic, or system of understanding and explanation. The bearing of this on Richard Adams' work is brought out in this famous passage by Ernest Hemingway, who like Adams is seeking 'empathic knowledge' not even of other humans, but of animals, in this case a lion.

The lion still stood looking majestically and coolly toward this object that his eyes only showed in silhouette, bulking like some super-rhino. There was no man smell carried toward him and he watched the object, moving his great head a little from side to side. Then watching the object, not afraid, but hesitating before going down the bank to drink with such a thing opposite him, he saw a man figure detach itself from it and he turned his heavy head and swung away toward the cover of the trees as he heard a cracking crash and felt the slam of a .30–06 220-grain solid bullet that bit his flank and ripped in sudden hot scalding nausea through his stomach. He trotted, heavy, big-footed, swinging wounded full-bellied, through the trees toward the tall grass and cover, and the crash came again to go past him ripping the air apart. Then it crashed again and he felt the blow as it hit his lower ribs and ripped on through, blood sudden hot and frothy in his mouth, and he galloped toward the high grass where he could crouch and not be seen and make them bring the crashing thing close enough so he could make a rush and get the man that held it.*

It is an amazing passage, but Adams is hardly less amazing in the suddenness and truthfulness with which he presents the familiarly human to a pair of eyes which finds the object not just unfamiliar, but unintelligible:

They ran on and crept through the hedge. Hazel looked down at the road in astonishment. For a moment he thought that he was looking at another river–black, smooth and straight between its banks. Then he saw the gravel embedded in the tar and watched a spider running over the surface.

This is a small example of what Adams does so consistently and powerfully throughout his novel. In the very striking scene in which the last survivors of the gassed-out warren catch up with the group of refugees who left before the disaster, Captain Holly describes a bulldozer (the lapine for any noisy machine is 'hrududu'):

A great hrududu came into the field from the lane. It wasn't the one the men came in. It was very noisy and it was yellow–as yellow as charlock: and in front there was a great silver, shining thing that it held in its huge front paws. I don't know how to

* From *The Short Happy Life of Francis Macomber*, collected in Hemingway's *The First 49* Cape 1944, p 21.

describe it to you. It looked like Inlé, but it was broad and not so bright. And this thing–how can I tell you?–it tore the field to bits. It destroyed the field.'
He stopped again.
'Captain,' said Silver, 'we all know you've seen things bad beyond telling. But surely that's not quite what you mean?'
'Upon my life (said Holly, trembling), it buried itself in the ground and pushed great masses of earth in front of it until the field was destroyed. The whole place became like a cattle-wade in winter and you could no longer tell where any part of the field had been, between the wood and the brook. Earth and roots and grass and bushes it pushed before it and–and other things as well, from underground.'

This unusual capacity to present the familiar as terrifyingly unprecedented is what–to return to the question of values–I would most want children to experience in the book. For the ten-year-old reading Captain Holly's description knows what a bulldozer is; he is in the traditional relationship of child to pet or doll or Peter Rabbit; for once, in a world otherwise full of giant grown-ups, abrupt and arbitrary eventualities, fixed authorities, wide-open and hostile spaces, the child knows better than the hero. He can experience the rabbits' bewilderment while understanding what is going on. (The same thing is brilliantly and sickeningly done for adults by Golding in *The Inheritors*, the tale which follows the slaughter of a group of defenceless Neanderthalers by men with a bow-and-arrow technology. With Golding, however, Darwin and St Paul are called silently to witness that all this destructive evil was inevitable.) More impressively yet, Adams goes on to take us beyond the incomprehension of rabbits into the moment at which they think themselves outside what is hitherto thinkable. The first such moment arrives when the escaping rabbits come across a little stream called the Enborne and their group intellectual, a rabbit called Blackberry, works out how to use a loose plank as a boat. Similarly, when with the foresight provided by the novelist which we share with the heroes, we know that the punt is ready for their escape with the captured doe rabbits, and we see Hazel and company drawn away into the current of the river Test under the nose of the pursuing tyrant General Woundwort, we experience at once the familiar satisfaction of relief at the last-minute safety of our side and at the same time the pleasure of understanding the incomprehension of the enemy as in his eyes solid ground moves magically away out of his reach.

It is this knot between *how* we see and the intellectual and verbal mechanisms we have for telling us *what* we see which Adams so vividly unties and ties again; to put it more technically, the central structure of the book builds and rebuilds the intricate, intercellular relations of perception and cognition, of image and idea. It gives us–and 'us' includes children–a strong, clear picture of how culture develops, and it does this broadly and simply in a dozen different ways. At one moment, Adams notes in an aside that rabbits cannot count beyond four, after that numbers blur into 'lots'; that the seagull Kehaar classifies 'all insects as beetles'–only their edibility is significant; or at another, Fiver, the seer, struggles with the idea of shaking meaning and its sounds out of 'the black sticks [which] flickered on the white surface' of a noticeboard as 'they raised their sharp, wedge-shaped little heads and chattered together like a nestful of young weasels'; a little before, we experience with the rabbits, the stupefying glare of a car's headlights, the 'awful brightness [of which] seemed to cut into the brain', and in all these and many other instances we are made to know the strangeness and omnipotence of an alien human technology, or else we are made to recognise the singularity and, as one might say, *interestedness* of our systems of concepts and the percepts which are a consequence of the concepts. Adams unfixes and refixes★ in the way only a novelist can the fluidity of experience, the facts of an intelligent eye and a brain which has to shape the world for the eye to see. This movement from dissolution to coagulation of ideas is sustained in play with the slow growth in the hero-rabbits' community of a dynamic culture. Hazel and company leave a static society, adroit and intelligent enough in its own way–its leader gives all the eerily familiar political reasons for not seeing crisis as crisis–and gradually construct a frame of thought capable of extension and adjustment, and of resistance and rejection too. Even from the doomed warren, larder to the farmer, they learn to carry and store food. They learn, against all their nature and their instincts, to travel long distances, to fight when they have to and not to run away from cats and dogs and foxes, they learn architectonics or how to build piered and vaulted underground halls, they learn friendship and dependence when their instinct is to scatter in a rout. These are the strengths of the book, that it insists upon the protracted difficulty of making a home out of exile, a society out of a gang of scared, forlorn, hungry bits and pieces, order and ceremony out of a sandy hilltop, a ride of sweet turf, and the cover of the tall pine trees. Culture is made out of the hard years, out of the permanence of fear, the threat of desert places:

Rabbits above ground, unless they are in proved, familiar surroundings close to their holes, live in continual fear. If it grows intense enough they can become glazed and paralysed by it–*tharn*, to use their own word. Hazel and his companions had been on the jump for nearly two days.

This is the broad moral of his task, and when it issues in generalisation then, for all Dr Adams' slight pomposity of manner, it rings true enough. In the long paragraph which opens Chapter 22, he reconnects the analogy between rabbits and communitarian (i.e. non-individualist) primitive peoples.

★ Compare Richard Gregory's two classics on perception *Eye and Brain* (1966) and *The Intelligent Eye* (1968).

Rabbits (says Mr Lockley) are like human beings in many ways. One of these is certainly their staunch ability to withstand disaster and to let the stream of their life carry them along, past reaches of terror and loss. They have a certain quality which it would not be accurate to describe as callousness or indifference. It is, rather, a blessedly circumscribed imagination and an intuitive feeling that Life is Now...

...Hazel and his companions had suffered extremes of grief and horror during the telling of Holly's tale. Pipkin had cried and trembled piteously at the death of Scabious, and Acorn and Speedwell had been seized with convulsive choking as Bluebell told of the poisonous gas that murdered underground. Yet, as with primitive humans, the very strength and vividness of their sympathy brought with it a true release. Their feelings were not false or assumed. While the story was being told, they heard it without any of the reserve or detachment that the kindest of civilised humans retains as he reads his newspaper. To themselves, they seemed to struggle in the poisoned runs and to blaze with rage for poor Pimpernel in the ditch. This was their way of honouring the dead. The story over, the demands of their own hard, rough lives began to reassert themselves in their hearts, in their nerves, their blood and appetites.

And he goes on to modulate into bolder and, we may feel, justifiable and strong moral assertion:

Would that the dead were not dead! But there is grass that must be eaten, pellets that must be chewed, hraka that must be passed, holes that must be dug, sleep that must be slept. Odysseus brings not one man to shore with him. Yet he sleeps sound beside Calypso and when he wakes thinks only of Penelope.

The Homeric reference is typical of the man who so loads even the rifts between chapters with epigraphs from Congreve, Xenophon, Sidney Keyes, folksong, Clausewitz, Robinson Jeffers. Adams is a manly man, and none the worse for it. But to say so brings me to the point at which his special limitations must be named. For the strong, rich, savoury presence in this novel which comes from its cultural ancestry in western literature seems to run, however strongly, into some very stereotypical forms.

In the first place, Adams is up against the structural difficulty of any anthropomorphic story-teller. He gives rabbits consciousness, which they do not have, but keeps them as rabbits. It won't do simply to say, with Richard Boston,[*] that Germaine Greer would hate the book because the female rabbits are simply there to bear children and to dig burrows while all the real friendships and human qualities are shown by the men. Adams' creation of an alien set of values and ideas out of which to see the world resists our making the novel into an animal fable; it is not the *Nonne Preeste's Tale* nor is it *Animal Farm*.

The kind of ideas that have become natural to many male human beings in thinking

[*] *The Guardian*, 6 August 1976.

of females–ideas of protection, fidelity, romantic love and so on–are, of course, unknown to rabbits, although rabbits certainly do form exclusive attachments much more frequently than most people realise. However, they are not romantic and it came naturally to Hazel and Holly to consider the two Nuthanger does simply as breeding stock for the warren. This was what they had risked their lives for.

But the difficulty for the novelist, as it is for anthropologists or any other scientist of understanding, is to find a way of telling what is unknowable in a known language. To do this he must give rabbits language and consciousness, and he must make these both inhuman and intelligible. The trouble with this sprawling, immoderate, unreflective book is that Adams has such an uneven touch in making such a language. He is by turns clumsy, portentous, longwinded, and magnificent. What makes the book into an unprecedented bestseller is this quite adventitious happiness of mixture.

There is, as they say, something for everyone. For the intellectual child or adult there is the rabbit lore, the creatively non-positivist animal behaviourism, and there are the makings of other cultures. Crossing into this territory, there is the ecology and the heady stuff of the conservation polemic, lapsing at times into an involuntary parody of *The Observer Book of Wild Flowers*. Woven into this thick technicolor, with all its living detail and the samples pasted in from the author's commonplace book, is the war thriller. Richard Boston has very amusingly ripped out this structure for anatomising, and mocked the 'onion-seller French and organ-grinder Italian' of Kehaar and 'maquis mouse'. Certainly the main group of rabbits are portioned out with a haversack of iron moral rations which would look best in a commando sortie: 'leadership for you, Hazel'; 'brainbox for you, Blackberry'; 'Bulldog Drummond kit for you, Bigwig'; 'nervous loyalty for raw recruits, Pipkin'; 'mad poet's outfit to Fiver'–'now, who's for a futile gesture?' But the success of any book for children in part depends on a single moral structure and a rattling good yarn; its strength and its weakness and, because of both, its sales, depend on having hit the right moment with this cultural recipe.* It is a depressing consequence of such success that as Adams becomes a more accomplished writer, if *Shardik* is anything to go by, the limitations of his mind and his imagination, once his ambitions draw him away from that simple, honest morality, leave him with nothing but the fashionable camp of Aztec cruelty, of a slow, ceremonious, picturesque, and brocaded dose of the horrors.

With *Shardik* we enter the world of *She*-in-the-seventies, a world in which *Equus*, *Rollerball*, and the wardrobe epics of regal serials on colour television combine to make their special, irresistible appeal to prurience, crass psycho-

* See also Graham Hammond's excellent essay in *Children's Literature in Education*, Vol 12, Spring 1973.

logism, cruelty, and sentimentality. These are among the grisliest imaginative expressions of the new interest in the occult, hallucinogens, mysticism, and the more phoney marginalia of the communards and alternative cuisine.* *Watership Down*, however, remains in the older, better tradition with which I began and joins forces with the best of the new, with the effort to understand relative truths from the inside and, above all, to see the world as wonderful.

That is why this essay links *Watership Down* to *A Wizard of Earthsea*. Both books return the world to the spellbinder. They coincide with the dissident impulse in old and new frames of thought to celebrate and to understand without disenchantment the creative powers of natural life in all its forms. I don't mean that both writers recommend their readers to think only calm, soothing thoughts and healing, life-giving ones like P G Wodehouse's poet; there is quite enough that is bleak and deadly in both authors. But both join that traditional activity of the storyteller, talking to children at play and to old men in the chimney corner, in that they seek to bind the world in spells of language. Adams does so as part of the history of making a culture; Ursula LeGuin goes back to the nature of language itself, its deep magic roots in experience, and intends to carry children back to those unquenchable sources.

She is, after all, an anthropologist and the daughter of anthropologists, the human science above all. She makes language, as it always was and is for Magi, the special preoccupation of her hero—intellectual. She sends him to university–the island of Roke–and she makes access to learning the slow, difficult initiation by rite and discipline which for an intellectual it must be. She makes thought a rare vocation, which it is, although she fails to add that those so called to the vocation take the thought in trust for others (the phrase tells); a proper wizard is both a man of the people who look up to him, *and* he serves the human mind and its unique responsibility towards the 'living principle' which is given form and regulation in language. The deep truth which it has become the manifold purpose of so much human inquiry these past fifty years to explore is that language and its infinite cognates–meaning, speech-act, statement, judgment, grammar, lexis, gesture–are not so much the key to all mythologies as the only order of things,† the only point at which to catch the coincidence of the Many and the One.

So Miss LeGuin's sorcerer learns at great pain the knowable names of things. At about the same time as she wrote her strange novel, a UCLA PhD

---

* Best and sympathetically charted and criticised by Theodore Roszak in *The Making of a Counter-Culture* Faber, 1970 and *Beyond the Waste Land* Faber, 1973.

† I take the phrase from Michel Foucault's *The Order of Things: An Archaeology of the Human Sciences* Tavistock, 1970.

student called Carlos Castenada* was writing a strange dissertation. In *The Teachings of Don Juan* and *A Separate Reality* Castenada describes the collision between the modern academic frames of thought and those of a Mexican Indian Magus. In the context of that collision with all its naïve adventuring, its picturesque and shimmering invocation of old magic, Castenada decides to drown the books of the academics and prefers the books of his masters:

Ye Elves of hils, brooks, standing lakes and groves,
And ye, that on the sands with printlesse foote
Doe chase the ebbing-Neptune, and doe flie him
When he comes backe: you demy-Puppets, that
By Moone-shine doe the greene sowre Ringlets make,
Whereof the Ewe not bites: and you, whose pastime
Is to make midnight-Mushrumps, that rejoyce
To heare the solemne Curfewe, by whose ayde
(Weake Masters though ye be) I have bedymn'd
The Noone-tide Sun, call'd forth the mutenous windes,
And twixt the greene Sea, and the azur'd vault
Set roaring warre: To the dread ratling Thunder
Have I given fire, and rifted Joves stowt Oke
With his owne Bolt: The strong bass'd promontorie
Have I made shake, and by the spurs pluckt up
The Pyne, and Cedar. Graves at my command
Have wak'd their sleepers, op'd, and let 'em forth
By my so potent Art. But this rough Magicke
I heere abjure: and when I have requir'd
Some heavenly Musicke (which even now I do)
To worke mine end upon their Sences, that
This Ayrie-charme is for, I'le breake my staffe,
Bury it certaine fadomes in the earth,
And deeper then did ever Plummet sound
Ile drowne my booke.

The importance of Ursula LeGuin in the reading experience of children is that she gives to our ancient conviction that language is magic both experience and theory. She complements the *practical* experiencing of alien and incomprehensible ideas in Richard Adams by showing how to experience these theoretic origins. Ged follows Prospero.

If this seems a mouthfilling claim to make for children's books, better such claims than the vaporous project work on *A Wizard of Earthsea* reported by Geoffrey Fox and his correspondents in the Advisory Service.† However

---

* *The Teachings of Don Juan* Penguin, 1970; *A Separate Reality* Penguin, 1973; *Journey to Ixtlan* Bodley Head, 1973. Also M Douglass *Implicit Meanings* Routledge, 1975, pp 193–200.

† See G Fox 'Notes on Teaching *A Wizard of Earthsea*', and J Cheetham 'Quarries in a Primary School' in *Writers, Critics and Children*, G Fox, *et al.*, Heinemann, 1976.

good their intentions, teachers with 'moly and thyme, yarrow and rushwash' (*Wizard*), dried, pressed, and made into birthday tokens, are doing nothing but turn the book into the humanities workcard; playing with a tarot pack and chanting primary school spells turns children into incipient, winsome folklorists of the brown-rice-and-dung-coloured-pinafore school. Ursula LeGuin is a lesser novelist, for children or adults, than Richard Adams, although, as I said, she has more sense of form and, in the narrow meaning, of art. She too–along with so many children's novelists, and along with a temper of the times–gives her narrative bold and alluring outline by making it relentlessly picturesque. With Yeats, she wants to make 'a great magic book of the people', to simplify landscape to cold stone and thorn, character to hawklike and sinewy purpose, eschatology to the self, pitching in the huge swell of empty seas. Time and again, her brief, rapid, striking tale gets on to the stilts of the epic movie–'the great oars shot out...the rowers bent their strong backs', and a Goodies pastiche:

'I do not understand.'
'That is because my lord Benderesk has not been wholly frank with you. I will be frank. Come sit by me here.'

Never mind. The best events in these books–the first and last splits which Ged causes in the universe, the last defeat of the dragons, the two passages through the valley of the shadow of death, the rescue of the mistress of Atuan, these are pieces of grand storytelling. But the larger moral climate is more abstract and austere. Mary Douglas' account of Castenada fits much of Ursula LeGuin's frame of thought and reference.

The last book ends with two old sorcerer-saints recalling their lives. They have been splitting their sides with laughter at elaborate jokes at the expense of their pupil. Then, replying to his questions, they look back on a long tale of withdrawal from worldly delights and sadness overwhelms them. One by one they have rejected the comforts of friendship for the sake of holding to their hard-won knowledge. They know that all doings are unreal: 'to hinge yourself on to either one is a waste of time because the only thing that is real is the being in you that is going to die. To arrive at that being is the not-doing of the self.'*

Adams' rabbits are indomitable doers; but as with Ursula LeGuin's it is the human understanding embodied by the book which concerns us. This is not to say that children's fiction is just a propaedeutic for social science (what a dreadful thought: 'here, have a dose of Marx with your *Tale of Ginger and Pickles*'). It is, however, to reaffirm that the novel as written for anybody is

* *Implicit Meanings*, p. 200.

an astonishingly inclusive and expressive way to render the changes in our consciousness of history and geography, of politics, and of our selves. As I have professed, these novelists are far from perfect, and there is in any case no guarantee that their readers–and for the purposes of this essay it doesn't matter if their readers are children or grown-ups–will see the point of all that is going on in the novels. As always, the business of criticism is to seek out the life of novels or films or television programmes or any other form of imaginative life, and to ask what are the values which give it that life, and what is the nature of the space between those values and ours. That Ursula LeGuin's trilogy and Adams' *Watership Down* stand up, as they do, for wizards, rabbits, and the intellectual life of either is an occasion for rejoicing at a time when intellectual life gets a pretty poor press, especially amongst school children.

Books by Richard Adams

Watership Down Rex Collings, 1972 (Carnegie Medal)
Shardik Allen Lane, 1974
The Tyger Voyage (with N. Bayley) Cape, 1976

Non-Fiction

Nature through the Seasons (with Max Hooper) Kestrel Books, 1975

Books by Ursula LeGuin

Books for Children include:

A Wizard of Earthsea Gollancz, 1971
Tombs of Atuan Gollancz, 1972
The Farthest Shore Gollancz, 1973
A Very Long Way from Anywhere Else Gollancz, 1976

Ivan Southall, *Josh* and the Persecution of Children

by

ALIX PIRANI

A SENSITIVE but by no means feeble city boy goes to visit his great-aunt in a little township out in the wilds 100 miles from Melbourne, a township founded by his great-grandfather. He tries to relate to the community of children and adults there, but in spite of an ostensibly hospitable welcome he becomes the object of persecution by the tough local children and comes close to being killed by a revengeful and thoughtless young mob.

This is the story of *Josh*: a nightmare story, but for adolescent or older readers not beyond what is possible in our own society. How do we confront that and come to terms with it in a real way, not dismissing it as only a nightmare, only a story? The novel offers us just that confrontation without any evasion.

It is written with an immediacy and realism that are compelling: a faithfulness to the character of the good-humoured, curious, intelligent schoolboy whose experience gives us the story, a vitality of event and of conversation, a clarity of time and place. Real as it is at this level, however, with all the aliveness of its young hero, there is at the same time a 'deadly' seriousness in it, the awareness of threat and of issues much more far-reaching. Readers may think they are in for a 'slice of life', and they are; but as they go on life turns out to be a good deal more than they might have imagined.

Ivan Southall is indeed absolutely in touch with real life, with our world and our children's world as it is, and at the same time he is part of a moral and spiritual tradition that seeks to make sense of life, to evaluate it, to understand what an individual's world is and might be. The tension between these two kinds of awareness is the essential energy of his writing.

Aunt Clara emerging from her boudoir all done up like a dog's dinner. 'Ready?'
'Yes, Aunt Clara.' A lie if ever there was one.
Opening the front door to the sunken porch with garden steps waiting to be climbed to the street-level gateway. Like mounting a platform to be exposed to public ridicule.

Kids of all kinds imagined lurking behind bushes, peering out of sunflowers, digging each other in the petals. 'Here's another Plowman dolled up in his Sunday pretties. What a prune. What a poppy.' They'd be there doing their sniggering. He knew all about country kids; they were as tough as old leather.

The complexities and subtleties, pains and joys of growth into a baffling society with values and conditioning that seem to thwart growth are presented against a natural background that itself offers boundlessness and also threat. The underlying question is: What can a man do, Nature and human nature being what they are? What is his potential? This is young Josh's problem in the 1930s as it was his great-grandfather's at the turn of the century; Josh's answers are significantly different.

I've written elsewhere* of the strengths shown in Southall's earlier writing. *Josh* seems to me to bring together all those strengths in a unique culmination, and I can only give here some indication of the richness of the novel; for besides being at a realistic level a vivid re-creation of the tensions and personal problems of our own lives–adults and children–it is an exploration of archetypal psychological truths, and an allegory based on the story of Christ, which is re-interpreted and extended anew. Southall is a religious writer in the best sense.

His books about children aren't solely for children any more than Dickens' or Mark Twain's were. Like Dickens, he isn't likely to be read by children–particularly those not familiar with the Australian background–without help and encouragement, because the style is not simple and the complexity of events, though always exciting, requires a considerable attention by the reader if it's to make more than a superficial impact. Unfortunately these days there isn't the family audience Dickens could write for: a book with a fourteen-year-old hero and an awareness expressed in a fourteen-year-old's language is allocated to the children's market. This novel is making profound statements about children, adults, and the journey into maturity, about society and its values, about responsibility, destructiveness, and power. Like *Great Expectations* it's a book in which a youth's view of his own growth to adulthood becomes a comment on the adult world.

Indeed, to say a book is 'difficult for children' is to beg the question of what children are, and the significance of Southall's work lies in his understanding that the distinctions once made between children and adults are no longer relevant: growth and maturing, we can now accept, happen or don't happen all through life.

Everyone up there at the gate; Aunt Clara apologising, apologising, apologising to everyone in sight.

* Ivan Southall. 'Writers for Children' *Use of English*, Vol 22, No 3, Spring 1971.

No one told me the match was so important. I thought it was a kid's game. Grown-up umpires. People coming to watch. I couldn't have played anyway. It's out of my class. What's wrong with Aunt Clara? Push, push, push. I didn't tell her I was a champion. I only told her I played. Wasn't that good enough?

Perhaps we've simply moved from the Victorian belief that every child is a diminutive adult to a belief that every adult is an overgrown child.

Josh, then, confronts life. And Josh, having confronted persecution, decides at the end of the book to get away and back to Melbourne immediately. It's the nature of that decision, the way it's arrived at and carried through, the kind of stature Josh has at this point, that make the book important, more than a nightmare story. He doesn't go as a coward; nor full of blaming and self-righteousness; but with a sense of his own responsibility in the affair, of how he became a victim and partly accepted it, and how he won't accept it in the future: he opts for life.

Significantly, Josh decided to visit his great-aunt of his own free will, in spite of friendly discouragement from his parents. So, at the beginning of the story, he has chosen himself, out of a kind of blind faith, to assert his connection with the Plowman family tradition; he thereby puts himself in a position of subservience and isolation.

The shock of reality is immediate. Aunt Clara waiting for him 'had the Plowman look, as if the railway station belonged to her, as if the earth had been made by her'. She takes him to the archaically ornate Plowman homestead and it's a confrontation with the tradition, and the confrontation also of an individual child with a powerful adult. A relationship in which he is a victim is immediately established—by her insistence, arrogance, and self-certainty, and her power as provider of food and shelter. Josh is disorientated, stripped of clothing, invaded, exposed, starved of the foods he likes (much in the manner of the institutions described in Goffman's *Asylums*)—and all this in a cheerful way by a 'nice old lady'. He protests, but to little effect.

This relationship established (an extreme but not atypical adult-child relationship), Josh emerges into the wider world of his peers, to find a totally baffling situation in which his hardly wanted relationship with his aunt, his being a Plowman, sets him apart from the Ryan's Creek children, who seem to respect the aunt, but resent, envy, and hate the nephew with a virulence he cannot comprehend nor account for. He cannot satisfy her wish that he be nice to them, nor their wish that he be non-existent (an extreme but not atypical inter-sibling relationship).

The Ryan's Creek children, living off an impoverished land in a time of depression, are 'primitive' in a way which shocks Josh's urban civilised feelings. In a crucial incident where they trap and cruelly kill a rabbit he amazes them by weeping; yet he sees how much he feels identified with the victim and how little he is prepared to own the 'accessory' inside himself who eats rabbit and who let the boys take his stick to use to kill this one. He sees too that he is more ready to cry for the rabbit, for others' pain, than for his own. He begins to learn from Bill, who is closer to nature, about the difference between rabbits and people.

This incident is one of several in which he begins to develop a growing sense of responsibility, self-awareness, and self-assertion. Paradoxically though, he continues to attract attack because he won't stay down. And each time he trips and falls on the unfamiliar ground–either literally or metaphorically– he arouses the other children's lust for dominance. Symbolically he carries on his back the clumsy haversack full of old-fashioned unappetising 'wholesome' food Aunt Clara has given him, and this often pulls him down. His need to shed the pack, trample angrily on it, eat from it, share the food, let it go bad, vomit it up, reflects his ambivalent feelings towards the tradition and the aunt that nourish him and over-burden him.

Throughout his further encounters with the children, and with the railway bridge his great-grandfather built which enabled Ryan's Creek to come into being, Josh explores the nature of his moral responsibility and his potential as a man. In relation to the unattractive and clinging Laura he easily slips into a treacherous situation in which she becomes his victim, chiefly because he began by despising her. Vicious tale-telling Jimmy is a dangerous little blackmailer, playing on Josh's bad conscience with satanic skill: it takes Josh some time to decide how not to be his victim.

As a poet and dreamer Josh tries sometimes to escape from the harsh real world, sometimes to seek, like his great-grandfather, idealised solutions, sometimes simply to express his feelings and his sense of beauty and wonder. And always there is the bush, with its snakes and man-set traps, and the wide open plains–to escape to, die in perhaps, though ultimately he will determine to walk back home that way, however arduous it is, and to stay alive so that the vultures won't want him.

Josh's developing relationship with Aunt Clara is one chiefly of discovery and disappointment on his side, and a slowly growing but limited understanding on hers. As the humane, dependable, and gentle provider she helps him and relates best: she appreciates reading his 'shocking' poetry, which wasn't meant for her eyes, and she warms to his pain, his capacity for feeling, to the man who can cry. But as the impatient upholder of belief, tradition, and a code of behaviour, constantly pushing him into moral commitments, she is to be fought with–either openly or in Josh's mind, where a dialogue with his aunt is often pursued. The first crisis between them comes when he confronts her with questions about her relationship with the children. What he doesn't know is that she is paying for the education of three of them. This has been hushed up by everyone like some guilty secret, and she does not reveal it to Josh even now. She evades the whole issue of their hatred, insisting that Josh go back and take part in a cricket match they have planned which he senses will be disastrous for him. This evasion, her refusal to see that her philanthropy causes hostility, means that she will not accept responsibility for the hatred–and Josh has to take the hatred for her. Her behaviour pitches him into violent frustration and anger, which he takes out inevitably on one of the youngsters: the confusion and violence grow until all sense of proportion is lost and Josh's reasons for being there at all are forgotten; the cricket match is cancelled; the adults aggravate matters by their blindness and narrow morality and, after keeping in his room, determinedly and hopefully out of the way, Josh emerges and is set upon by both teams.

He is beaten, ducked, nearly drowned. After his recovery Aunt Clara speaks warmly and gratefully of the *catharsis* this event has brought to troubled Ryan's Creek. Still unwilling to admit fully that her benefactions have caused and will continue to cause bad feeling, she now reassures Josh that everybody wants to accept him and he can really enjoy the last few days of his stay. Josh, however, knows better than his idealistic aunt and leaves immediately for home, refusing to allow himself to be used any longer. He shows the sort of strength a contemporary boy hero must find–it is similar to Lenny Hawk's at the end of Barry Hines' *The Blinder*, the ability to say no to an adult world which wants to make child heroes, a world which expects its children to act out its own unsolved problems and fantasies: the unproved and unrewarded idealisms and moralities, or the violent anger, suppressed and denied, at the absence of reward, the frustrations of a deeply unsatisfying way of living. All parents expect this, to some degree, of their children; maturity comes when a child realises this is happening and rejects it. Some children never achieve this and in the circumstances it may not matter. But in a society which is as confused, blind, morally bewildered and unstable as ours, young people are confronted sharply with the mess their elders are putting on them; they must make choices and decisions in order not to become victims to the past. It is their revaluation of the tradition and their only hope for a better future.

Josh makes his rejection: rejects the moral pressure, rejects, in this context, the narrowness of a world-view based on life in a small depressed community; his horizons are larger. He rejects the old Christian ethic his aunt adheres to, the fierce Old Testament morality of Ryan's Creek which lies behind her attitude to her nephew. As Joshua he might have inherited the mantle of Maximilian Plowman, who never saw his Promised Land. But the Promised Land being an illusion, all that was left was for Josh to be the Messiah. So she has pushed him into the role of martyr. He has played his role exactly and has explored, through this experience, a concept of Christian morality he now outgrows. This outgrowing is his 'rising' again, with a new significance, a moral and spiritual understanding for our time.

Josh has learned about evil and seen that it is inseparable from good: that there is always resentment of the Giver and the Gift which is conditional but life-vital. The Giver might be God, Nature, mother, benefactor: what Josh has to reject is the pretence that the Giver is clean and clear of all responsibility or badness. He muses, after some talk with his aunt, about God and men:

...What about me when I was a little kid out in the sun pouring boiling water on ants crawling over the front step? What a horrible thing to do. Even Mum couldn't have cared. Where would I have got the kettle from? She must have known what I was at. Can I cry for little ants too? Can I cry now because I didn't cry then?
You can play hymns on your organ and for you that makes it right.

The spiritual truth that Josh finds himself asserting is that God is Process, is what happens; not some kind of unreachable ideal in whose interest we smooth over the facts of our real life with all its unfairness, destructiveness, and ironies. This smoothing over is, pertinently, what many people want children's writers to do: Southall has received his share of criticism on that score. Josh the poet is, like his creator, a realist: an agent, participant, and observer of process. He transcends an older generation's view of the poet as chiefly observer: he 'cries for himself'; feels the pain, goes beyond 'turning-the-other-cheek', the defence against showing one's pain in real personal contact which is characteristic of men of words and sermons. For his creator Josh achieves a fusion of the man of action and reality with the man of poetry and dreams: the split is perhaps more marked in Australia than here. There is a gulf between young Harry, typical pioneer, tough and hardworking, heavy with blind and guilt-based morality and good intentions in a deprived world, and Josh, humane, sensitive thinker, more civilised, sophisticated, broadminded. The gulf is bridged when Harry finally breaks violently with his fists through the imagined pride and callousness of the dreaming Plowman to find a weeping and hurt boy whose baffled detachment, involvement, and strength are quite different from what he had decided. Two humans see one another. Josh survives his fear by staying with the pain instead of running away. Yet his 'don't care' is still there and significant. It puzzles Harry. It is the necessary detachment, not of callousness, but of self-protection, based on a candid valuing of oneself as much as others. Like Blake's Little Boy Lost, who says 'Nought loves another as itself'–and is promptly sacrificed by the horrified 'Priestly care', Josh is aware that genuine love of oneself affects one's sense of responsibility for others, and knows how dubious are the motives from which Aunt Clara imposes her gifts on others, how ambivalent was his own attitude to Laura. Crying for others is not enough. Out of an honest 'don't care' we can begin to care; live our own lives instead of trying to live other people's.

At the same time, while Harry learns the quality of Josh's detachment, Josh learns the quality of Harry's aggressiveness. It is straight, a complete release, and once paid out, finished; and he takes full responsibility for it. It is very different from Josh's own blind lashing out at Bill, messy enough to leave him thinking 'doing things physically is not my way'. Very different too from the mob violence which later follows, and from which Harry tries to protect him.

What can Josh do with all this awareness, this new knowledge of himself? How, growing up, is he to be a man and manifest his potency? His self-important great-grandfather built a railway bridge whose intention was to bring civilisation to the wilds–all it produced was dead-end Ryan's Creek. The bridge in itself is a beautiful achievement, a fine structure, but its high ideal was not to be: indeed it was responsible for the very situation which is anything but civilised for Josh. Josh's own power will be in the beauty of structure in poetry rather than in stern idealism: in concern with process and direction and reality rather than with invisible and idealised goals. What he shares with Aunt Clara's father, as she recognises, is a basic humanity, imagination, the power to feel, and a capacity for trust; these seem to emerge as the important part of the Plowman tradition–though Josh's trust will never be so blind, nor turned into rigid self-injunction.

It is characteristic that Aunt Clara is a not entirely reliable interpreter of her father's tradition, that she does the idealising, and looks on him, and hopes to look on Josh, as more than human. The women and girls in the novel are all potentially misleading to Josh in their desire to push him (as Laura does) into a position of responsibility he doesn't want, or push other boys and men into positions of tyrannical power, egotistical or self-martyring authority. This has to be resisted by a confused Josh who only wants their love, beauty, understanding. Betsy is the one he admires but she is a willing slave to a bullying Harry. This passage is central to the story:

Josh bewildered, bewildered, moaning inside, fighting to stop it from showing. They were accusing him of things they were inventing. 'It's not true. You kids couldn't pick the truth if you heard it. Why don't you ask Betsy about the cricket? Betsy, it wasn't like that, was it? It's the same with everything. Not like you say. I couldn't be that stupid. You must be talking about some other fellow.'

Rex giggling and Betsy looking at the ground and Harry giving his pants a hitch. 'Don't you turn up for cricket. You dig yourself a hole and crawl down it. If it wasn't for your auntie I'd flatten you now. I'd *flatten* you, Joshua.'

Harry walking away like an ape, Rex going with him tossing pebbles between his hands, Betsy still standing in her pool of shadow, eyes downturned.

'Betsy.' Josh saying it sadly.

Betsy glancing at him and drooping from the shoulders as if her head had become heavy, Josh suddenly wondering, but Harry was at the cemetery gate, waiting. 'Come on, Betsy. What are you doing?'
'Betsy, I haven't told any tales, not about anything, I swear it.' Wanting to go after her as she walked away, but afraid of Harry. 'Betsy, I didn't tell Laura to jump off the bridge, I swear it. What really happened wasn't anything like it. Where do they get these stories? And I didn't threaten that little kid without a jolly good reason. He's a horror. Betsy, why did you let Harry think those things about the cricket? Are you scared of him or something?'
But she had left him to it and he was talking to the trees.
Gosh, Josh, you're letting them wipe the floor with you. You'll have to go in with your fists swinging; it's the only thing they'll understand. All this nobleness and sweetness; they don't think that way. Dob 'em in, Josh; you can't be the martyr for ever. That Laura! Why protect her? What do you think you're proving? That there's a fool born every minute and every one is you?
Josh wandering back to Great-grandfather's grave to reread the inscription.
He always gave his fellow man the benefit of the doubt.
'If it's true, Great-grandfather, you're a better man than I am.'

The accusations and inventions that Harry had loaded heavily on him before this were all twisted half-truths that a weak Betsy could accept. Harry probably believes them: they are projections of his own guilty feelings. One of the horrifyingly lifelike qualities of the novel is the constant projection of paranoid feelings by one Ryan's Creek character on another, to produce a situation in which persecution of an outsider is almost inevitable. At times Josh is utterly bewildered by the others' mishandling of words.

Nevertheless the novel isn't all 'horror'. The tone is set by Josh's awareness: his stream of consciousness, poetic and rhythmically powerful at times, is wryly observant, humorous, self-critical, dramatic.

To anyone wishing to explore the parallel with the story of Christ the detail is fascinating, never forced, richly illuminating. Finally Josh goes beyond. As Piers Plowman woke from the dream to the real world, so Josh Plowman survives his nightmare. His plan is to make the difficult walk home, experiencing the way for himself rather than using the railway track laid down by others. So Jesus is alive and well and enjoying the journey to a more open future. How easily can a world bred in a tradition based on the virtue of martyrdom and suffering accept that?

Books by Ivan Southall

Books for Children include

Meet Simon Black Angus and Robertson, 1950
Simon Black in Peril Angus and Robertson, 1951
Simon Black in Space Angus and Robertson, 1952
Simon Black in Coastal Command Angus and Robertson, 1953
Simon Black in China Angus and Robertson, 1954
Simon Black and the Spacemen Angus and Robertson, 1955
Simon Black and the Antarctic Angus and Robertson, 1956
Simon Black Takes Over Angus and Robertson, 1959
Simon Black at Sea Angus and Robertson, 1961
Journey into Mystery Landsdowne-Angus and Robertson, 1961
Hill's End Angus and Robertson, 1962
Rockets in the Desert Angus and Robertson, 1964
Indonesian Journey Landsdowne-Angus and Robertson, 1965
Ash Road Angus and Robertson, 1966
To the Wild Sky Angus and Robertson, 1967
The Fox Hole Methuen, 1967
The Sword of Esau Angus and Robertson, 1967
Let the Balloon Go Methuen, 1968
The Curse of Cain Angus and Robertson, 1968
The Sly Old Wardrobe Cheshire-Angus and Robertson, 1968
Finn's Folly Angus and Robertson, 1969
Chinaman's Reef is Ours Angus and Robertson, 1970
Bread and Honey Angus and Robertson, 1970
Josh Angus and Robertson, 1971 (Carnegie Medal)
Head in the Clouds Angus and Robertson, 1972
Over the Top Methuen, 1972
Matt and Jo Angus and Robertson, 1974
Seventeen Seconds Brockhampton, 1974
Fly West Angus and Robertson, 1975

The Historical Novels of
Rosemary Sutcliff

by

JOAN V MARDER

'...A STIMULUS to the imaginative and critical faculties and an education in human sympathies.'* These are the qualities which Professor Helen Cam finds in the best historical novels for adults; the qualities which adults seek in the books they choose to place before children; and the qualities which are to be found in the historical stories of Rosemary Sutcliff. Much has already been written about her work, and her books have set a standard by which contemporary historical novels for children are judged. Her books are praised for the quality of historical imagination which they reveal, for the language in which they are written, and for their excellence as novels. They are not, in the main, easy books, and the children who enjoy them are those with considerable reading ability and enthusiasm for books, but, to these children, they give a deep and lasting enjoyment.

Miss Sutcliff's first book, a retelling of the Robin Hood legends, and the three which followed, are written for younger children and, while they give pleasure, they do not suggest the range and power of the later books. Signs of this developing potential came with the publication of *Simon* in 1953, a story with a Civil War setting, whose hero fights for the Parliamentary cause. Teachers welcome this book as a counterweight to the over-romantic view of the war seen from the Royalist camp which is commonly propounded in historical novels; but to the child reading the book, it is very much more than a *roman à thèse*, it is a story about timeless and enduring problems. Simon, the name character, has to resolve the rival claims of friendship and loyalty to a cause, to grow up and to move from the protection of his family to an adult life with public responsibilities. This blending of historical setting and timeless problems is the mark of all Rosemary Sutcliff's later work, and one of the main reasons for its popularity with children. Professor Kenneth Charlton suggests that 'the primary urge of children to read any book is for the gratification of their emotional needs, a satisfaction

* H Cam *Historical Novels* Historical Association, 1961, p 3.

138

based largely on their being able to identify with one or the other of the characters of the book'.* This possibility of identification, this externalisation of the preoccupations of young people growing up in a troubled and dangerous world, makes a very direct appeal, ensuring that the books are relevant to their readers, not mere escapist literature.

In the year after *Simon* appeared, *Eagle of the Ninth* was published, and marked the beginning of a sequence of novels which explore many aspects of Roman Britain from the full flush of Roman power until long after the legions had departed, and Rome was only a memory and a hope in the hearts of a few men–a civilisation, a way of life, 'the last brave glimmer of a lantern very far behind'. In each of the novels, the hero has his personal conflict, his particular quest. Aquila, in *The Lantern Bearers*, has to overcome the bitterness left by the destruction of all he held dear in his youth and to learn the importance of personal relationships and the value of family love. Owain, in *Dawn Wind*, keeps his ideal of Roman civilisation before him through all his years as a Saxon thrall, and he too discovers the importance of his obligations to his fellow-men. Phaedrus, in *The Mark of the Horse Lord*, wins his freedom in the arena and, with Roman fortitude, gives his life for the safety of the tribe which had made him their lord. These and other heroes express the adolescent's need to work out a code of behaviour, to discover his public loyalties, and to establish his personal integrity.

Beside the Romano-British sequence, there are three novels which explore similar personal problems in different historical settings. These are: *The Shield Ring*, a story of the Norse community in Lakeland which maintained its freedom and way of life for a generation after the Norman Conquest; *Knight's Fee*, set in Norman Sussex; and *Warrior Scarlet*, set in Bronze Age Sussex. Perhaps even more strongly than in the Romano-British novels, the reader is aware of the theme of quest, of overcoming handicap, of the adolescent's urgent need to play his part in the life around him. Drem, in *Warrior Scarlet*, has the handicap of a crippled right arm. Society's demands are uncomplicated and uncompromising. To take his part in the life of the tribe, he must kill his wolf in ritual battle and be able to take his place in the warrior band; if he cannot fulfil these demands, then he must be banished to live with the conquered Neolithic people, the shepherds and servants of the tribe. Randal, in *Knight's Fee*, is physically whole but spiritually crippled–abandoned as a baby, he has learned to keep alive by lying and stealing–and he has to learn a more ordered way of life. For both Drem and Randal, the major problem is to conquer their handicap, to learn not to allow resentment to colour their relations with their fellows, and to give and accept friendship.

To the history teacher, Rosemary Sutcliff's novels are a valuable teaching

* K Charlton *Recent Historical Fiction for Secondary School Children* (11–15 years) Historical Association, 1960, p 4.

aid. The novelist's imagination illuminates and brings to life periods and ways of life that are remote and difficult to understand. Norman land-tenure is a complex study, but the rights and duties of knight-service are the very stuff of the plot of *Knight's Fee*, as is the Romanisation of Britain in such books as *The Silver Branch*, *The Lantern Bearers*, and *Dawn Wind*. We are today cushioned from the elements, but Rosemary Sutcliff can make us feel the famine that lurked at winter's end, the threat of wolves making each winter night dangerous. We can feel the narrow boundaries, the constriction of the tribal world, or the stretching of the known world under the Roman Empire. The impression of space, of the difficulties of journeying from one settlement to another, and the time consumed in doing so, come with a shock of surprise to the child of today's world of easy transport; to one growing up in this overcrowded island.

In recent years we have come to demand, as a matter of course, that historical novels should be free from anachronisms; but teachers who wish to make use of such books need a more positive quality than mere absence of error. In Rosemary Sutcliff's work, they should find this positive contribution. A study of local history, an investigation of the tangible remains of the past, are both ways in which history can be invested with a feeling of reality for children, but the good historical novel also has a part to play. Historians can follow a closely reasoned argument and can emerge with a coherent picture, but this is asking for a mature judgment and an already awakened feeling for history. For children, the novelist's imagination, transmuting the minutiae of daily life and the political arguments of long ago, can strike the spark which may lead to further investigation and understanding.

'An education in human sympathies'—these novels certainly provide this. We may, in carping mood, wish that some things were different—the male characters are much more memorable than the women in the books (but, on the whole, men did take most of the adventures for themselves), and the books are of a complexity which puts them out of the reach of many children. This is an ungrateful complaint, for no book can be all things to all men, and we should be glad of books which will extend and, at the same time, delight our more intelligent children.

(1968)

Books by Rosemary Sutcliff

Stories for Children

The Chronicles of Robin Hood OUP, 1950
The Queen Elizabeth Story OUP, 1950
The Armourer's House OUP, 1951
Brother Dusty-Feet OUP, 1952
Simon OUP, 1953
The Eagle of the Ninth OUP, 1954
Outcast OUP, 1955
The Shield Ring OUP, 1956
The Silver Branch OUP, 1957
Warrior Scarlet OUP, 1958
The Lantern Bearers OUP, 1959 (Carnegie Medal)
Knight's Fee OUP, 1960
Beowulf Bodley Head, 1961; reprinted as *The Dragon Slayer* Puffin, 1966
Dawn Wind OUP, 1961
The Hound of Ulster Bodley Head, 1963
The Mark of the Horse Lord OUP, 1965
The Chief's Daughter Hamish Hamilton, 1967
The High Deeds of Finn MacCool Bodley Head, 1967
A Circlet of Oak Leaves Hamish Hamilton, 1968
The Witch's Brat OUP, 1970
Tristan and Iseult Bodley Head, 1971
The Truce of the Games Hamish Hamilton, 1971
The Capricorn Bracelet OUP, 1973
The Changeling Hamish Hamilton, 1974
We Lived in Drumfyvie (with Margaret Lyford-Pike) Blackie, 1975

Non-Fiction

Rudyard Kipling Bodley Head, 1960
Houses and History Batsford, 1960
Heroes and History OUP, 1965
A Saxon Settler ('People of the Past') OUP, 1965

Bibliography

Further Reading

Joan Aiken

'A Thread of Mystery' *Children's Literature in Education*, Vol 2, July 1970

L M Boston

Margaret Meek 'A Private House' *Times Literary Supplement*, 15 June 1973. Reprinted in *The Cool Web* Bodley Head, 1977
Jasper Rose *Lucy Boston* Bodley Head Monographs, 1965
'A Nip of Otherness' *Children's Literature in Education*, Vol 6, 1971

Alan Garner

'Alan Garner's Elidor' *Children's Literature in Education*, Vol 7, March 1972
'*Red Shift*–Some Aspects Considered' *Children's Book Review*, Vol 4, Summer 1974

Cynthia Harnett

'Stories not history: the historical novels of Cynthia Harnett' *Children's Literature in Education*, Vol 9, November 1972
'Cynthia Harnett–A Tribute on her Eightieth Birthday' *The Junior Bookshelf*, Vol 37, August 1973

Russell Hoban

The Times, interview by Philippa Toomey, 15 November 1974
Hard Times 2, University College, Cardiff, interview by John Archer, December 1974
The Guardian, interview by Alex Hamilton, 24 March 1975
Newsweek, 4 August 1975
'A narrow pavement says "Walk Alone": the books of Russell Hoban' *Children's Literature in Education*, Vol 20, Spring 1976

William Mayne

'On the Littoral: William Mayne's *The Jersey Shore*' *Children's Book Review*, Vol 3, October 1973
'Chorister Quartet' *Signal*, Vol 18, September 1975

Mary Norton

Fred Inglis *Ideology and Imagination* CUP, 1975
G Josipovici *The World and the Book* Paladin, 1973
P Laslett *The World We Have Lost* Methuen, 1971
'Mary Norton and the Borrowers' *Children's Literature in Education*, Vol 7 1972

Philippa Pearce

'The Novels of Philippa Pearce' *Children's Literature in Education*, Vol 4, March 1971

K M Peyton

'The Carnegie Medal–A Speech of Acceptance' *The Junior Bookshelf*, Vol 34, October 1970
'The Flambard Trilogy: Objections to a Winner' *Children's Literature in Education*, Vol 8, July 1972

Ivan Southall

Ivan Southall *A Journey of Discovery: On Writing for Children* Kestrel Books, 1975
'Teenage Fiction–a close look' *Books for Your Children*, Winter 1969–70

Richard Adams

'Musings on *Watership Down*' *Books for Your Children*, Vol 8, August 1973
'Some Ingredients of *Watership Down*' *Children's Book Review*, Vol 4, Autumn 1974. Reprinted in *The Thorny Paradise*

Ursula LeGuin

'High Fantasy: A Wizard of Earthsea' *The Horn Book*, Vol 47, April 1971
'*A Wizard of Earthsea* and the Charge of Escapism' *Children's Literature in Education*, Vol 8, July 1972

Rosemary Sutcliff

M Meek *Rosemary Sutcliff* Bodley Head, 1962

General Studies

There are many books and surveys of the history of children's literature, but the following are particularly useful:

F J Harvey Darton *Children's Books in England* 2nd edition revised, Cambridge, 1970

Cornelia Meigs *et al. A Critical History of Children's Literature* Macmillan, New York, 1964

J R Townsend *Written for Children* revised edition, Penguin, 1974

G Trease *Tales out of School* revised edition, Heinemann, 1964

On Modern Children's Literature

The most useful of recent studies concentrating mainly on writing since the 1950s are:

E Blishen *The Thorny Paradise: Writers on Writing for Children* Kestrel, 1975. Among those included are Joan Aiken, Leon Garfield, Philippa Pearce, K M Peyton, Richard Adams, and Ursula LeGuin

Eleanor Cameron *The Green and Burning Tree, On the Writing and Enjoyment of Children's Books* Atlantic Monthly Press, Boston, 1969. Especially good on time fantasy and Lucy Boston

Sheila Egoff (ed) *Only Correct: readings in children's literature* OUP, 1969. An attractive collection of essays including Edmund Leach on 'Babar's civilisation analysed', and Lillian Smith on 'Criticism'

Frank Eyre *British Children's Books in the Twentieth Century* Longman, 1971

Margery Fisher *Intent Upon Reading—a critical appraisal of modern fiction for children* revised edition, Brockhampton, 1965. An extraordinary survey combining breadth with readability

Virginia Haviland *Children and Literature* Bodley Head, 1973. A useful collection of essays including Lillian H Smith's 'An Approach to Criticism of Children's Literature'

Wallace Hildick *Children and Fiction* Evan Brothers, 1970. A study of the factors involved in writing for children

Peter Hollindale *Choosing Books for Children* Elek, 1974. A balanced survey of the problems

Fred Inglis *Ideology and the Imagination* CUP, 1975. A study of education and politics, but with two challenging chapters on children's books

J R Townsend *A Sense of Story: Essays on Contemporary Writers for Children* Longman, 1971. Essays and book lists on nineteen contemporary writers including Joan Aiken, Lucy Boston, Leon Garfield, Alan Garner, William Mayne, Philippa Pearce, K M Peyton, and Ivan Southall

F Whitehead, A Capey, and Wendy Madron *Children's Reading Interests* Schools Council Working Paper 52, Evans/Methuen Educational, 1952

Justin Wintle and Emma Fisher *Pied Pipers: Interviews with influential creators of children's literature* Paddington Press, 1974. Includes Joan Aiken, Leon Garfield, Alan Garner, and Richard Adams